Choosing Life in Christ
A Vocation to Holiness

A Retreat
(Part of *The Art of Spiritual Life* Series)

Edward Kleinguetl

outskirts
press

Man stands between God and nothingness, and he must choose.

—Pope St. John Paul II

Age-old experience in academic theology has shown
convincingly that it is possible to acquire wide [scholarship]
in the science of theology without having a lively faith—
that is, in a condition of total ignorance of God. In such
cases theology becomes an intellectual profession ...

—Elder Sophrony of Essex

Here on earth there is nothing that can give us inner peace.
For neither riches, nor glory, nor honor, nor position, nor
family, nor neighbors can give us unshakeable inner peace.
There is only one giver of life, peace, and joy—God.

The Lord permits many disappointments, sorrows, and
misfortunes to befall us in this earthly life in order that we
might stop placing our trust in the world, which harms
us so much, and that we might realize that he alone is
the Source of all comfort, peace, and stillness.

—Elder Thaddeus of Vitovnica

IMPRIMATUR

+ Daniel Cardinal DiNardo, DD
Archbishop of Galveston-Houston
October 9, 2019

For His Grace Bishop Milan Lach, SJ of the Eparchy of Parma,
who answered the call of Christ to follow him,
said "yes" to serve in the United States,
is committed to the spiritual renewal
of the Byzantine Catholic Church,
and believes his first priority as a bishop
is to teach people how to pray

Table of Contents

The Choice

"If it does not please you to serve the Lord,
choose today whom you will serve ..."
(Joshua 24:15)

"There are two ways: one of life and one of death—
and there is a big difference between the two."¹
(Didache 1:1)

"It is time for us to become a spiritual people again."
(Matthew Kelly)

Opening Reading

Read: Deut. 30:15-20 (The choice before Israel) or

Josh. 24:14-15 (Choose today whom you will serve) or

Matt. 6:24 (No one can serve two masters).

The Choice

There is Good News! Despite the difficulties and confusion in our midst, there is a message of hope, the Gospel of Jesus Christ, who lived, died, and rose that we would be set free from sin, death, sorrow, inner emptiness, and loneliness.² Many messages of the secular world try to

---

1   *The Didache: The Teaching of the Twelve Apostles*, transl. R. Joseph Owles (North Charleston, SC: CreateSpace, 2014), 1. The Didache is an important historical document of the Early Church, written in the first century, which includes teachings on the Christian life, virtue, Christian ethics, Church rituals (Baptism and Eucharist), and Church organization.
2   See Bishop Joseph E. Strickland, Diocese of Tyler, comments at the USCCB Meeting, November 13, 2018. https://www.youtube.com/watch?v=gsURjhLkvTg.

drown out or dismiss the relevance of faith, however, it is this Good News that gives us hope in an atmosphere of pessimism and uncertainty.

Christ is the true light who came into the world, and darkness cannot overcome it. He is near to us. He will show us the path to the abundant life God promises us. We just need to make the radical decision to follow him, to more clearly recognize his presence as our guide and teacher, allowing his light to pierce the darkness in our lives. In turn, as authentic Christian disciples, we help lift up a fallen world in need of healing.

As Catholics, we are beneficiaries of a faith that is ever ancient, ever new, handed down to us for generations since the time of Christ. Faith matters. The message of the Gospel is as relevant today as it was to the people to whom Christ ministered in ancient Israel. He gives us hope and tells us of a Father in Heaven who loves us beyond all our imagining. Our journey here on earth is to make our way back to him, to share in the abundant life he intended for us.[3]

There was a time when it was easy to be a Christian. As Archbishop Fulton Sheen (1895-1979) said, "The atmosphere was Christian; morals were Christian; there was no great problem adapting ourselves to a Christian society."[4] Today, as Christians, we can no longer simply blend in or follow the crowd, because our society is moving in a different direction. So we are either swept along with the current, or we hold steadfast to our convictions. What was once cultural is now counter-cultural, and we need to make a choice as to the path we will follow. There is no middle way. Fair warning: our decision to follow Christ may not be politically correct and may place us in the minority.[5]

"Jesus could not make it any clearer: following him requires our

---

3   See John 10:10. All biblical quotes contained herein are from the NABRE, 2011, unless otherwise specified.

4   See Joseph Pronechen, "Archbishop Sheen's Warning of a Crisis in Christendom," *National Catholic Register*, online (July 29, 2018), 3.

5   See Matt. 7:14. "How narrow the gate and constricted the road that leads to life. And those who find it are few."

all."[6] Consider the experience of the Christians of the Early Church, who were also in the minority.

> The believers of the first century felt the constant social pressure to compromise their faith by worshipping the emperor in cult worship, tolerating false teachers, and leading lifestyles that mirrored the pagan world around them.
>
> Has anything much changed ...?[7]

The Church was built on a foundation of witness and sacrifice. The Early Christians also had to make a choice and this often meant risking one's life. Tertullian (ca.155-220), an early Latin theologian, wrote, "The blood of Christians is seed (of the Church)."[8] He essentially said that the willingness to sacrifice leads to the conversion of others. And it is because of these sacrifices, as well as those throughout the centuries, our Catholic faith has been transmitted down to our present age.

Today, however, we cannot help but notice a cooling of faith in the world around us. And, as faith diminishes, we also notice a corresponding listlessness, a lack of purpose, and people striving to find happiness that seems so elusive. Many feel empty inside. As C. S. Lewis wrote, "All that we call human history ... [is] the long, terrible story of man trying to find something other than God which will make him happy."[9] So we need to consider this: if "something other than God" fails to fulfill the human spirit or provide us the lasting happiness we seek, perhaps it is time to take a renewed look at what God has to offer. In short, the reason fullness and happiness elude us is because we strive to fill infinite longing, the longing God

---

6   Madeline Arthington and Karrie Sparrow, "What Happened to the Seven Churches of Revelation?" *International Mission Board* (June 1, 2018), 11. www.imb.org.

7   Ibid.

8   Tertullian, *Apologeticum*, no. 50. Taken from "Tertullian's Defense," transl. Rev. S. Thelwall, ed. Dan Graves, www.christianhistoryinstitute.org/study/module/tertullian.

9   C. S. Lewis, *Mere Christianity* (New York: Macmillan, 1952), 53.

created within every human person, with finite things or temporary distractions. Only God is infinite; only he can fill our infinite longing. So, how can we determine God's plan and purpose for our lives? How do we find happiness and fill our deep, innate sense of longing?

The only true way to know God's plan for us is by coming to know and love his Son, Jesus Christ, who modeled for us a right-ordered relationship with our Heavenly Father. Every human heart consciously or unconsciously seeks this truth.[10] However, the truth we seek can only be found in Christ, choosing to live the life he modeled for us. This choice leads us to the eternal blessedness God promises[11] and to a greater sense of wholeness and completeness. "When religion does not give people an inner life or a real prayer life, it is missing its primary vocation."[12]

Let us seek Jesus and examine his message to us—God's personal invitation to share in his blessedness.[13] Let us consider the difference of a God-centered life versus one that is constantly chasing after the world and all its empty promises. In turn, we must choose the path we will follow. One is darkness and death; the other, Light and Life.

As we enter into this retreat, let us also keep in mind four fundamental questions:

1. Who is Jesus Christ?

2. How do we come to know and love Jesus Christ?

3. How does Jesus Christ teach us to live a good and moral life?

4. How are we called to become missionary disciples of Jesus Christ?[14]

---

10 See John 8:31-32: "If you remain in my word, you will truly be my disciples, and you will know the truth, and the truth will set you free."

11 See John 10:10.

12 Richard Rohr, OFM, "Breathing Under Water," *St. Anthony Messenger* (August 2019), 38.

13 See 2 Pet. 1:4.

14 Daniel Cardinal DiNardo, Archbishop of Galveston-House, "A Catechetical Framework for Lifelong Faith Formation," promulgated on August 6, 2013. These four themes are to be the foundation of all faith formation within the archdiocese.

These are essentially the themes from the four conferences of this retreat, and these questions will provide the basis for our ongoing reflection as we discern our decision to follow Christ. Let us rediscover the spiritual tradition of the Church leading us to Christ. Bear in mind, discipleship is serious stuff and requires an unrelenting commitment.[15]

Icon of the Resurrection.

We are asked to make a choice. Let us consider what Jesus tells us: "I am the way and the truth and the life. No one comes to the Father except through me" (John 14:6). With this in mind, let us consider the wisdom of Elder Porphyrios, who said, "When people are empty of Christ, a thousand and one other things come and fill them up: jealousies, hatreds, boredom, melancholy, resentment, a worldly outlook, worldly pleasures. Try to fill your soul with Christ so that it's not empty."

---

15   Arthington and Sparrow, "What Happened to the Seven Churches of Revelation?", 11.

CONFERENCE NO. 1

The Call[16]

"Come after me ..."
(Matt. 4:19)

"The invincible desire of every man is holiness. God himself
implanted in the heart of man this unceasing divine yearning"[17]
(Monk Moses of Mount Athos)

Opening Gospel Passage

Read: Matt. 4:18-22 (The Call of the First Disciples).

Defining Vocation

"Follow me." We know well the story of the calling of the first apostles. They left everything to follow Jesus. We equate this story with vocation and often we think this is only about a call to the priesthood, or to become a monk or a nun. However, if this is our reaction to the story, we are missing a critical point.

True, the word "vocation" comes from the Latin "calling." One specific definition is "a divine call to God's service or to the Christian life."[18] Yet, that does not limit the calling to priesthood or the monastic life. The "Christian life" is God's invitation "to share in the divine nature,"[19] to the blessedness of life in the Holy Trinity. It is God's wish

---

16 This conference and its theme recurring throughout this retreat was greatly influenced by a homily of Fr. Miron Kerul-Kmec, St. Nicholas Byzantine Catholic Church, Barberton, Ohio (June 23, 2019). https://artofspirituallife.podbean.com/e/june-23-2019-1561584878/.

17 Monk Moses of Mount Athos, *Holiness: Is It Attainable Today?*, transl. Fr. Peter A. Chamberas (Brookline, MA: Holy Cross Orthodox Press, 2012), 8.

18 "Vocation," www.dictionary.com.

19 2 Pet. 1:4.

to save each person, because we are all made in the divine image. We are all called to a vocation of holiness, to share in eternal life. We are called to be saints, to be saved, and to be redeemed—no exceptions! That is why in the Early Church, there was no differentiation between the spirituality of clergy, religious, and laity—all have the same calling to share in eternal blessedness.

How do we bring this vocation to life? The Gospel passage for this conference provides us with an answer. These fishermen heard Christ say, "Follow me." They made the radical decision to follow Jesus, leaving everything behind. The Gospel points out that two of these men, James and John, even left their father, Zebedee, in the boat. They said "Yes" to God's voice without hesitation.

Jesus's command, "follow me," is heard throughout the Gospel. Jesus was God's personalized invitation to call all people to himself. His offer of eternal life is completely gratuitous, reflective of God's overflowing love for us: He knocks at the door of our hearts[20] and "he will not rest until he has moved us from the gutter to the Palace."[21]

Let's consider "follow me" in the Gospel context. In Matthew, Chapter 8, we learn of Jesus preparing to depart for the other side of the lake.

> A scribe approached and said to him, "Teacher, I will follow you wherever you go." Jesus answered him, "Foxes have dens and birds of the sky have nests, but the Son of Man has nowhere to rest his head."
>
> Another of [his] disciples said to him, "Lord, let me go first and bury my father." But Jesus answered him, "Follow me, and let the dead bury their dead."[22]

---

20 See Rev. 3:20. See also John 15:23.
21 Anthony M. Coniaris, *Tools for Theosis: Becoming God-like in Christ* (Minneapolis: Light & Life Publishing Company, 2014), 80.
22 Matt. 8:18-22.

Or, we can consider the story of the rich young man in the Gospel of Mark:

> As he was setting out on a journey, a man ran up, knelt down before him, and asked him, "Good teacher, what must I do to inherit eternal life?" Jesus answered him, "Why do you call me good? No one is good but God alone. You know the commandments: 'You shall not kill; you shall not commit adultery; you shall not steal; you shall not bear false witness; you shall not defraud; honor your father and your mother.'"
>
> He replied and said to him, "Teacher, all of these I have observed from my youth."
>
> Jesus, looking at him, loved him and said to him, "You are lacking in one thing. Go, sell what you have, and give to [the] poor and you will have treasure in heaven; then come, follow me."
>
> At that statement his face fell, and he went away sad, for he had many possessions.[23]

Contrast the responses of the scribe, the disciple, and the rich young man to that of the fishermen, who left their livelihood behind; James and John even left their father. Similarly, consider the call of Matthew:

> As Jesus passed on from there, he saw a man named Matthew sitting at the customs post. He said to him, "Follow me." And he got up and followed him.[24]

A certain irony begins to unfold in the Gospel. Those whom society would have deemed "holy," the scribe and the rich young man

---

23 Mark 10:17-22.
24 Matt. 9:9.

(wealth at the time of Jesus being considered a blessing for a virtuous life), struggled with Jesus's call, "Follow me." Yet those deemed to be sinners (a tax collector) and the uneducated, working class of society (fishermen) had little problem making such a radical choice. Further, Jesus makes it clear: "No one who sets his hand to the plow and looks to what was left behind is fit for the kingdom of God."[25] In other words, we need to choose this vocation to holiness and stick with it. We cannot straddle the fence between Jesus and the secular world. Jesus's invitation is unambiguous: "Come after me."[26]

Jesus also makes it clear that he provides the way to eternal life[27] and tells us, "If anyone wishes to come after me, he must deny himself and take up his cross daily and follow me."[28] Again, there is a constant focus on *following* Jesus.

Bringing the Vocation to Life

The radical decision to follow Christ is only the first step of our vocation to holiness. Consider how the apostles' choice unfolded. These men spent three years with Jesus—being formed and taught by him, and observing his example. The Gospels reflect that formation, memorializing the teachings and actions of Jesus for others to follow.

It is also important to note that the apostles were not perfect. They failed. They were often shown to be weak in faith (consider Peter when he walked on the water[29]). James and John were ambitious, wanting to sit at the right and left of Jesus in his kingdom.[30] The disciples fled in fear in the Garden of Gethsemane.[31] Peter betrayed

---

25 Matt. 9:62.
26 Matt. 4:19.
27 See John 14:6. Jesus said to him, "I am the way and the truth and the life. No one comes to the Father except through me."
28 Luke 9:23.
29 See Matt. 14:22-33. Jesus says to Peter, "O you of little faith, why did you doubt?" (Matt. 14:31). Note that Jesus did not say Peter had no faith. Rather, his faith in Christ was not yet perfected.
30 See Matt. 10:35-37.
31 See Matt. 26:56. "Then all the disciples left him and fled."

Jesus, denying him three times.[32] When all seemed lost, only John was with the women at the foot of the cross.[33] Thomas doubted the resurrection.[34] After the crucifixion, the apostles were scared, hiding behind locked doors.[35] One could argue three years of formation by Jesus were for naught. Yet, when the Holy Spirit came at Pentecost, the formation bore tremendous fruit: the Church was born. Further, as we read in the Acts of the Apostles and Epistles, we can understand what Life in Christ is truly like: it is the abundant life he promised.[36]

Consider what this vocation to holiness means and how we bring it to life. First, we must have the courage to say "yes" to Jesus, to accept his invitation, and follow him. However, this is just the beginning. We must remain steadfast, not looking to what was left behind.[37] If we are half-hearted in our vocation, we will be losing life—almost akin to hemorrhaging. Those near us also will begin to lose life and, often, hope. For example, if we are parents and do not work on our vocation to holiness, our souls will begin to die and we will be unable to pass this life on to our children. We cannot give what we ourselves do not have. If we only give God part of our life, we must not expect to attain eternal blessedness. "He takes into account the measure of our surrender to him."[38]

In many cases, the choice will not be easy because the secular world has a glitzy marketing campaign, trying to persuade us what we need to find happiness and fulfillment. Many of us who have pursued this fruit, which appears so appealing and good, have found it to be thoroughly rotten inside. This is the nature of self-will and sin:

---

32   See Matt. 26:31-35, and 69-75. At the Last Supper, Peter said to Jesus, "Though all may have their faith in you shaken, I will not deny you" (Matt. 26:33).

33   See John 19:25-27.

34   See John 20:25. "Unless I see the mark of the nail in his hands and put my finger into the nailmarks and put my hand into his side, I will not believe."

35   See John 20:19. "[T]he doors were locked, where the disciples were, for fear of the Jews...."

36   See John 10:10.

37   Cf. Matt. 9:62.

38   Archimandrite Sophrony Sakharov, *We Shall See Him As He Is* (Platina, CA: St. Herman of Alaska Brotherhood, 2006), 104.

"The woman saw that the tree was good for food and pleasing to the eyes, and the tree was desirable for gaining wisdom."[39] This is how sin appears to us, filled with empty promises, pleasing to the eye, tempting us. So, we must choose: Christ—or the secular world and its empty promises, life or death. There is no middle way.[40]

The journey toward personal holiness is one filled with challenges. We need to follow Jesus intentionally, remain in his presence, and allow him to form us. The Spiritual Fathers and Mothers who have gone before us will tell us the journey is a constant struggle. We must strip away everything that keeps us from entering more deeply into relationship with Christ. However, if we persevere, we will discover a greater fullness and contentment. We will find inner peace, even in the midst of severe trials or challenging circumstances.

In our vocation to holiness, we also have to create the right environment and consent to living in Christ, to remain in his presence. He says to us, "Be with me.[41] Let me lead you,[42] guide you,[43] teach you.[44] Let me give you strength.[45] Surrender yourself to me[46] and I will take care of everything."[47] Further, the more we empty our hearts, especially of self-will and our own desires, the more God can fill

---

39   Gen. 3:6.

40   Sakharov, *We Shall See Him As He Is*, 110.

41   Consider both the call of Jesus, "Come, follow me" (Matt. 4:19), and remaining connected to him as the Source of Life: "Remain in me" (John 15:4).

42   See Luke 9:23, "If anyone wishes to come after me, he must deny himself and take up his cross daily and follow me." Also, consider Jesus's final words to Peter: "You follow me" (John 21:22). Jesus wants to lead us to the Father.

43   See John 14:6. "I am the way and the truth and the life. No one comes to the Father except through me."

44   Consider Luke 6:40. "No disciple is superior to the teacher; but when fully trained, every disciple will be like his teacher." Our objective in following Jesus is to become more Christ-like (*theosis*), to prepare ourselves for eternal blessedness (union with God in heaven).

45   See Matt. 11:28-30. "Come to me, all you who labor and are burdened, and I will give you rest. Take my yoke upon you and learn from me, for I am meek and humble of heart; and you will find rest for yourselves. For my yoke is easy and my burden light."

46   Consider John 14:23. "Whoever loves me will keep my word, and my Father will love him, and we will come to him and make our dwelling with him."

47   See John 14:1. "Do not let your hearts be troubled. You have faith in God; have faith also in me." Consider too the prayer from the Surrender Novena of Fr. Dolindo Ruotolo (1882-1970): "O Jesus, I surrender myself to you, take care of everything!"

them with his love.

Our vocation to holiness is about incremental change over time. In the Christian East, this incremental transformation is called *theosis*, which means that we become more God-like as we cultivate the virtues.[48] This brings us to another key point: We must constantly practice the virtues in our spiritual life and never give up. There are tools to assist us: prayer, Sacred Scriptures, the Church with its liturgy and Holy Mysteries. There are people, the Church Fathers and Mothers, who have gone before us and who provide us with tangible examples of following Jesus.

We can also expect to fail along the way. The apostles failed. Our Spiritual Fathers and Mothers struggled and failed. Yet, after failure, we get back up. We are never alone. Christ, the Theotokos, and all the saints pray for us and give us strength to continue. Their lives provide us with examples that we need, because many of the saints experienced struggles similar to our own. In this manner, we prepare ourselves to experience the blessedness promised by Christ, eternal life, to share in the very life of the Holy Trinity. This is true life. Anything else is death. As Elder Porphyrios of Kavsokalyvia (1907-91) tells us:

> Christ is life, the source of life, the source of joy, the source of the true light, everything. Whoever loves Christ and other people truly loves life. Life without Christ is death; it is hell, not life. That is what hell is—the absence of love. Life is Christ. Love is the life of Christ. Either you will be in life or in death. It's up to you to decide.[49] A Deep-seated Relationship

---

48 This transformation of becoming more God-like is also referred as divinization or deification.

49 Elder Porphyrios, *Wounded by Love: The Life and Wisdom of Elder Porphyrios*, ed. Sisters of the Holy Convent of Chrysopigi, transl. John Raffan (Limni, Evia, Greece: Denise Harvey, 2013), 97.

It is not unusual for a person to have a deep spiritual experience, to feel a burst of fire in one's heart. However, if we do not cultivate and tend this fire, if we do not remain in Christ and follow him intentionally, that sudden burst of faith will be smothered. It is like the Parable of the Sower and the Seed,[50] specifically the seed that fell on rocky ground:

> "It is like the one who hears the word and receives it at once with joy. But he has no root and lasts only for a time. When some tribulation or persecution comes because of the word, he immediately falls away."[51]

In this case, if we have no depth to our relationship with Christ, we will lose life. Further, if we become complacent in our vocation to holiness, we will gradually lose life and it will be easy to fall prey to temptation. That is why Jesus instructed his disciples,

> "Remain in my love. If you keep my commandments, you will remain in my love, just as I have kept my Father's commandments and remain in his love."[52]

This is the way to retain true life, to remain in Christ.

Creating a Fire Within

As we cultivate our vocation to holiness, remaining rooted in Christ, we begin to create a fire within ourselves. Consider the example of the disciples on the road to Emmaus.[53] They were dejected and defeated, their hope diminished. They lamented the absence of Christ ("we were hoping he would be the one"[54]). Yet contrast this

---

50   Matt. 13:1-9.
51   Matt. 13:20-21.
52   John 15:9-10.
53   Luke 24:13-35.
54   Luke 24:21.

sentiment to when they recognized Jesus in the breaking of the bread: "Were not our hearts burning within us?"[55] This encounter contrasts the difference of a heart absent Christ and one with Christ. The latter has a fire within.

As we cultivate our relationship with Christ, we feel warmth of heart, as many Spiritual Fathers have described it, and this fire can reach others. We bear witness to Life in Christ by making his priorities our priorities, by living as he would have us live, by having a future full of hope even in the midst of difficulties, and by loving God and loving our neighbor. As authentic disciples, we are called to share that Life in Christ with others, because God desires the salvation of all. As Jesus tells us:

> "I have come to set the earth on fire, and how I wish it were already blazing! There is a baptism with which I must be baptized, and how great is my anguish until it is accomplished!"[56]

It is up to each of us as authentic Christian disciples to keep the fire burning brightly. As contemporary Catholic apologist Matthew Kelly wrote, "How would the world be different if we Christians simply *behaved* as Christians? Imagine."[57] Imagine, indeed. Imagine the life that would flow forth from us—life that could be shared with others.

Choosing Christ in the Midst of Darkness

There is no question that we have seen much darkness in our world today. We have seen a significant cooling in the fervor of faith and many have left the Church. However, if we do not answer the call of Christ, if we do not say "yes," we will not have life. Only Christ is life. If we do not accept his invitation, we are like a branch separated

---

55 Luke 24:32.
56 Luke 12:49-50.
57 Matthew Kelly, *Rediscover Jesus* (North Palm Beach, FL: Beacon Publishing, 2015), 183.

from the vine.[58] Without Christ, we will be disconnected from the true source of life.[59] We will have despair and death, unhappiness and hopelessness, and a constant seeking for something that will fill our inner longing. How many people around us today are listless, drifting, and seeking for meaning in everything other than God? Perhaps we are the ones who find ourselves seeking or searching. To find life, the first step is to say "yes" to Jesus's invitation, "Follow me."

To be clear, the vocation to holiness is a constant struggle to stay the course, and we must consistently cultivate the soil so that the seed of faith implanted within us will bear much fruit. Our faith needs roots. Looking around today, many find life to be a drudgery; we look to fill that inner emptiness with pleasures or material things. We have lost interest. Joy eludes us. We question, "Are we really alive?" It is so easy for us to fall away from the practice of our faith when we become lukewarm, and this often leads to despair, depression, despondency, and even burnout. Yet rather than seeking elsewhere or blaming this on some psychological malaise, we should recognize such moments as times when God calls us to accept our vocation to holiness, to hear the sound of his Son's voice, "Follow me." Sometimes, God will allow our faithfulness to be tested in order to perfect it.[60]

If we are ever tempted to think we have failed, are unworthy of God's love or have done something that cannot be forgiven by God, consider the example of Peter. In his fear, he denied Jesus. Yet, Jesus redeemed his failings when he appeared to the apostles at the Sea of Tiberias and asked Peter three times, "Do you love me more than these?"[61] And what are the last words of Jesus to Peter—in fact, the

---

58   John 15:5. "I am the vine, you are the branches. Whoever remains in me and I in him will bear much fruit, because without me you can do nothing."
59   See John 15:45. "Remain in me, as I remain in you. Just as a branch cannot bear fruit on its own unless it remains on the vine, so neither can you unless you remain in me. I am the vine, you are the branches. Whoever remains in me and I in him will bear much fruit, because without me you can do nothing."
60   See Sakharov, *We Shall See Him As He Is*, 85.
61   See John 21:15-19.

last words of Jesus in the Gospel of John? "You follow me."[62] Jesus calls *all*, regardless of our failings. As St. John of Kronstadt (1829-1908) wrote, "What are your sins (no matter how bad they may be) compared to God's mercy, if only you truly repent?"[63]

Throughout the remainder of this retreat, we will consider further this vocation to holiness, saying "yes" to the call of Jesus, and persevering on the spiritual journey, by remaining in Jesus, learning from him, being strengthened and guided by him. In turn, this will deepen our relationship with Christ, and our lives will be incrementally transformed (*theosis*). However, at this point, simply think of Jesus's invitation: "Follow me."

Instructions for Personal Reflection

At the end of certain conferences, we will provide a short reflection to be read, alone and in silence. Based on the discussion in the conference and this reflection, consider the questions below.

Reflection for Conference No. 1 (Option No. 1, for Youth): The Story of Teresa[64]

> Teresa was a popular girl, a Julia Roberts look-alike who liked sports, guys, and parties. She was a varsity basketball player, and was voted homecoming and prom queen in her senior year. Thinking she had found true love, she entered into an unhealthy dating

---

62   John 21:22.

63   St. John of Kronstadt, *My Life in Christ*, Part 1, transl. E. E. Goulaeff. Revised and adapted by Nicholas Kotar (Jordanville, NY: Holy Trinity Monastery, 2015), 63. Consider the two thieves dying on the cross with Jesus (see Luke 29:39-43). One of the thieves mocked Jesus and the other repented, given the assurance that he would be with Jesus that day in paradise. The two thieves represent the fact that the offer of salvation is available to all, but not all will accept it.

64   Sr. John Mary, "A Life from Prom Queen to Cloistered Nun," http://www.passionistnuns. org/vocationstories/ findinglove/index.htm.

relationship with an abusive individual. This consumed three years of her high school life, but one day she finally ended the relationship—and felt relieved. Teresa then went to college in southern Indiana and liked the party scene. However, she also met a friend who was involved with the Catholic National Evangelization Team (NET). With her NET friend, she went to Steubenville and discovered a real desire to know Jesus. But she acknowledged you could find her one night at a prayer service at the Catholic student center and the next night at a big campus party. She felt the party scene was her ticket to happiness and true love. She wanted both worlds.

Yet the more Teresa tried to hold on to both, the more disillusioned she became by the party scene. In her heart, she knew she was drawn to Christ—everything else left her empty. Teresa wanted to find love. She was thirsting ...

God gave us the freedom to choose. We generally want the freedom to do what we like. We are free to judge, to look out for number one, to be self-centered, to be proud, to be boastful, to discriminate or belittle others, or to get our way, even if it requires force or coercion. Yet is this really freedom? Or, rather, is this enslavement to sin? The reality is that true freedom means constantly dwelling in God.[65] Only then are we truly free.

---

65   Cf. Archimandrite Sophrony Sakharov, *St. Silouan the Athonite*, transl. Rosemary Edmonds (Crestwood, NY: St. Vladimir's Seminary Press. 1991), 65.

Reflection Questions

1. Do I find myself thirsting in my own life? For what am I thirsting? Thirst is a metaphor: Consider it the deep-seated longing that we each have inside ourselves, that longing for "something," without knowing exactly what it is. It is the restlessness we all experience in our lives.

2. When I reflect on the invitation of Jesus, "Follow me," what do I think?

3. Do I seek Christ in my life? How do I experience him?

4. Consider the story of the Samaritan Woman at the Well (John 4:4-42). She had made mistakes in her life. She wanted love and could not find it. She was considered an outcast and was alone. Yet, here was Jesus sitting at the well … *specifically waiting for her!* Do I realize that Jesus is waiting for me too?

5. Have I experienced Jesus's call to me to follow him? What was the experience? Recall it in detail. How did I respond at the time? What was the outcome?

Reflection for Conference No. 1 (Option No. 2):

Christ asks us to follow him *unconditionally*. We generally do not have an issue with this, except when the spiritual journey runs into challenges or during times of trial. Think of Peter walking on the water and how he was seized with fear (See Matt. 14:27-32). It is in the storm when our faith is challenged, helping us to gauge whether our spiritual foundation is built on rock or sand. At times like this, some may second guess or desire to take control: "Thanks, God, but no thanks. I have a better plan."

Am I willing to follow Christ, even when his way is not my way or the way I think things should go? Do I truly trust in his plan for me?

Consider the example of St. Anna Schäffer (1882-1925). She was a German peasant woman who greatly desired to become a nun. An accident at a laundry left both her legs severely scalded. She remained essentially bedridden in a life of intense suffering, and was forced to abandon her lifelong dream of entering a religious order. However, Jesus confirmed to her that she would have to "suffer, sacrifice, and atone in silent secrecy." Accepting this condition—that God had a different plan for her life—her prayers became ever deeper and more substantial, sometimes leading into deep mystical experiences. She prayed for and strengthened many through her personal witness. Her apostolate consisted primarily of correspondence.

Are we willing to follow Christ even when his plans for us are different than our own?

Reflection Questions

1. Have I had a definitive experience of Jesus calling me to follow him? What was the experience? Recall it in detail. How did I respond at the time? What was the outcome?

2. Have there been times in my life when God's plan for me was different than my own plan? How did I react? Did I experience disappointment? Did I surrender? How did it work out? What did I learn from the experience?

3. Today, how do I seek to discern God's will for my life?

"The Call of the Apostles Peter and Andrew" by Duccio di Buoninsegna (National Gallery of Art, Washington, DC).

The first step in the spiritual journey is to say "yes" to Christ (Matt. 4:19) and make the radical choice to follow him, even when this decision is in contrast to the dominant culture. As Pope St. John Paul II (1920-2005) said, "Man is in the middle between God and nothingness, and he must choose."

Encounter

"... but he would withdraw to deserted places to pray"
(Luke 5:16)

"He who is able to pray correctly, even if he is the poorest of
people, is essentially the richest. And he who does not have proper
prayer is the poorest of all, even if he sits on a royal throne."
(St. John Chrysostom)

"Learn to love prayer. In order not to live in darkness, turn on the switch
of prayer so that divine light may flood your soul. Christ will appear
in the depths of your being. There, in the deepest and most inward
part, is the Kingdom of God. The Kingdom of God is within you."
(Elder Porphyrios)

Introduction to the Conference

In our first conference, we reflected on the invitation of Jesus, that we are each called to a vocation of holiness. He asks of us, "Be with me. Let me lead you, guide you, teach you. Let me give you strength. Surrender yourself to me and I will take care of everything." This requires us to have a personal relationship with Christ, not just intellectual acknowledgement of whom he is, but to truly remain with him. We need to experience his presence, which means we need to encounter him. To be clear:

> First and above all, God is personal. In fact, he is a
> communion of loving persons (the Most Holy Trinity).
> God is not an idea, or an ideology, or an equation,
> or magic, or a force, or an intelligent gas cloud, or
> a hypothesis. God is as real and as personal as you

and me—only much more so, because God is the source of personhood and author of reality. We can love a person and, being personal, God can love us back. We can't love a gas cloud, and ideas don't have relationships.[66]

This same God who created the universe, the God who is "ineffable, inconceivable, invisible, incomprehensible, ever-existing, yet ever the same,"[67] a God beyond all our imagining, desires a personal, intimate relationship with each of us. Our deepest longing can be fulfilled only by establishing a personal, intimate relationship with him.[68] This is God as Jesus has revealed him to us—a God who cares so much for us that even the very hairs on our head have been counted.[69] God's greatest desire is to draw near to us, and our journey through life is to make us accustomed to experiencing his presence. This type of relationship with God should be normal for all of us, not just for a select few. God wants to live with us now in this life, not just in heaven. Thus, encountering God is needed to develop a deeper relationship with him, to remain with him, and to be guided to him by his Son Jesus Christ.

There are numerous ways we can encounter Jesus, including the Church with its liturgical life and the Holy Mysteries (Sacraments), Sacred Scripture, and contemplative prayer. In fact, two components of the interior life, the sacramental life of the Church and personal

---

66 Archbishop Charles J. Chaput, OFM Cap., *Living the Catholic Faith: Rediscovering the Basics* (Cincinnati, OH: St. Anthony Messenger Press, 2001), 17.

67 From the Anaphora (consecration prayer) of the Divine Liturgy of St. John Chrysostom. *The Divine Liturgies of Our Holy Father John Chrysostom* (Pittsburgh: Byzantine Seminary Press, 2006), 72. See also Robert F. Taft, "The Authenticity of the Chrysostom Anaphora Revisited. Determining the Authorship of the Liturgical Texts by Computer," *Orientalia Christiana Periodica* 56(1) (1990): 28–29. Taft explains that Chrysostom (d. 407) used the Anaphora of the Twelve Apostles of Syrian (Antiochian) origin when he came to Constantinople and added phrases. This particular phrase was a genuine addition to the Anaphora by Chrysostom himself.

68 See Eph. 1:5–6. The God and Father of our Lord Jesus Christ "destined us for adoption to himself through Jesus Christ, in accord with the favor of his will, for the praise of the glory of his grace that he granted us in the beloved."

69 See Matt. 10:30.

prayer, were never intended to be separated. Together, they represent the fullness of the interior life.

Robert Cardinal Sarah (1945—) writes, "I would say that, for a Christian, faith is man's total and absolute confidence in a God whom he has *encountered personally*."[70] The crisis of faith we are experiencing today, particularly in North America and Western Europe, is not because organized religion has lost meaning, as some would like to argue. The crisis exists because many have lost or have not been exposed to one of the most fundamental components of our faith: the ability to encounter Jesus through prayer. Simply put, we as a Church and a society do not know how to pray as we should.[71] As Matthew Kelly writes,

> Nothing will change a person's life like really learning how to pray. It's one of life's most powerful lessons. And yet, astonishingly, we don't teach people how to talk to God. We don't teach them to pray with their hearts in a deeply personal way. It is one of the areas of singular importance where we have fallen short as a Church.[72]

Accordingly, while there are other means of encounter, our primary focus in this retreat will be on prayer. As St. John of Kronstadt wrote, "It is indispensable for every Christian to acquire the habit of turning quickly to God in prayer about everything, since we are weak, and he is the source of all power and goodness."[73] A current-day

---

70 Robert Cardinal Sarah, in conversation with Nicolas Diat, *The Day is Now Far Spent*, transl. Michael J. Miller (San Francisco, CA: Ignatius Press, 2019), 24. Emphasis added by author.

71 See Gabriel Bunge, OSB, *Earthen Vessels: The Practice of Personal Prayer According to the Patristic Tradition* (San Francisco, CA: Ignatius Press, 2002), 9. This monk describes the "evaporation of faith" and how, despite the best efforts, Christianity seems to be growing cold. His premise is that somehow we have lost touch with the importance of a personal prayer life which was always an essential part of the mystical tradition of the Early Church.

72 Matthew Kelly, *Rediscover the Saints* (Assam, India: Blue Sparrow Books, 2019), 31.

73 St. John of Kronstadt, *My Life in Christ*, Part 1, 57.

monk of Mount Athos would add: "Combined with inner purification and a regular sacramental life, a life of prayer will help significantly in the regeneration of the faithful during this difficult period in which we live."[74]

To put this into further perspective, St. Teresa of Calcutta (Mother Teresa) had a very simple philosophy: "Pray and trust." It is that simple and yet that hard because to trust someone, we must personally know him or her. To have a personal relationship with Jesus Christ, to come to love him and trust him above all else, we must come to know him through prayer. We must learn to truly pray.[75]

Opening Gospel Passage

Read: Luke 5:12-16 (Jesus cleanses the leper).

The Importance of Cultivating Prayer

Jesus was busy during his earthly ministry, and people were constantly seeking him. Yet no matter how busy he was, he always found time to withdraw for prayer, to spend time with his Father. We, too, need to make time for prayer, to remain in the presence of Jesus, to strengthen and sustain our vocation to holiness.

Fr. Mina al Macarius is a 91-year-old monk who spent the past 53 years as a hermit living outside the Monastery of St. Macarius in Egypt's Wadi al Natron. He only recently began accepting a few visitors at his hermitage. In the wisdom he shared with his visitors on April 1, 2019, Fr. Mina was quite empathetic: "Without prayer,

---

74 Monk Moses of Mount Athos, *Athonite Flowers: Seven Contemporary Essays on the Spiritual Life*, transl. Fr. Peter A. Chamberas (Brookline, MA: Holy Cross Press, 2000), 60.

75 See Evagrius Ponticus, *The Praktikos & Chapters on Prayer*, transl. John Eudes Bamberger, OCSO (Kalamazoo, MI: Cistercian Publications, 1972), 65. "If you are a theologian you truly pray. If you truly pray you are a theologian."

without Jesus, we have nothing."[76] He advised that we should daily recite with our whole heart, "Jesus, Jesus, I love you. Jesus, Jesus, I love you." Children, he said, are part of this; by age 10, they should learn to love Jesus. Prayer is critical to such a relationship.

The Living Jesus is meant to be experienced. It is through our encounters with him that personal transformation occurs and progress in our vocation to holiness. The busyness of our lives often takes away from time to cultivate a genuine rule of prayer. However, Jesus was a busy person too, constantly in demand, teaching people, and curing the afflicted of their ailments. Yet, he withdrew to deserted places to be alone with his Father, providing us with an example of how we need time to be refreshed and renewed, cultivating the divine presence within. Accordingly, we need to make time to create a relationship with God through prayer, to listen to his voice in silence and solitude.

Conditions for Prayer – Exterior and Interior Stillness

In our first conference, we spoke about remaining in the presence of God. We need to create the right environment in order to gain greater awareness of living in the presence of Christ. We need to flee the noise and busyness of the world through exterior and interior silence. St. John Climacus in his seminal work, *The Ladder of Divine Ascent*, describes this as a three-part process[77]:

First   Detachment from concern with regard to the necessary and unnecessary. This involves examining our own self-denial and withdrawal from the trappings of our lives. As St. John Climacus described it: "The first task of stillness is disengagement from every affair, good and bad, since concern with the former leads on to the latter."[78]

---

76 Fr. Mina al Macarius, April 1, 2019. Sharing his wisdom with a few visitors, including the author.
77 See St. John Climacus, *The Ladder of Divine Ascent*, transl. Colm Luibheid and Norman Russell (New York: Paulist Press, 1982), 268. Step 27, "On Stillness."
78 Ibid.

Second   Urgent prayer (experiencing a genuine need for prayer in our lives).

Third   Unremitting action of prayer in the heart, or "Prayer without Ceasing."

The Early Desert Fathers and Mothers in the third to fifth centuries withdrew into the wilderness to find an environment conducive to exterior stillness, which in turn would be conducive to interior silence. We, in turn, can learn lessons from this Desert Spirituality. While we may not be able to move to the desert, we can empty ourselves through ascetical practices, free ourselves from worldly attachments, unshackle ourselves from bitterness and anger, surrender our self-will to the Divine will—freeing ourselves from distractions—so we can similarly begin to cultivate the conditions for interior stillness. This calmness allows us to encounter God in prayer, to be filled by his presence. Jesus provided the example, withdrawing regularly to deserted places to be alone with his Father. The Gospel of Luke places particular emphasis on this aspect of Jesus's ministry, illustrating that prayer is "essential to the response of faith."[79]

Interior Stillness (*Hesychia*) and the Origins of the Jesus Prayer

Prayer and personal purification are required to produce the interior stillness referred to as *hesychia*. In turn, interior stillness provides the conditions necessary for encounter. However, the Desert Fathers and mothers also thought us that the encounter required a method of prayer. The origins of the Jesus Prayer evolved from the Desert Fathers and Mothers and this tradition has been faithfully practiced and preserved in the Christian East ever since. When asked by one of the brothers how one should pray, Abba Macarius (300-391) advised:

---

79   Luke Timothy Johnson, *The Gospel of Luke*. Taken from *Sacra Pagina* series, vol. III, Daniel J. Harrington, SJ, ed., (Collegeville, MN: A Michael Glazier Book, The Liturgical Press 1991), 24.

There is no need for long discourses. It is enough to stretch out one's hands and to say, 'Lord, as you will, and as you know, have mercy.' And if the conflict grows fiercer, say: '*Lord, help!*' He knows very well what we need and he shows us his mercy.[80]

Short, simple prayers were required to fix the mind on the presence of God. From the Gospels, the cry of the blind man on the road to Jericho was, "Lord, Jesus Christ, son of David, have pity on me."[81] The humble prayer of the publican was, "O God, be merciful to me, a sinner."[82] These became the prayers of the Desert Fathers and Mothers, along with the litany of the liturgy, *Kyrie eleison* ("Lord, have mercy"). St. John Cassian (360-435), who spent time with the monks in the Egyptian desert before heading to the West, described in his *Conferences* his particular prayer: "Come to my help, O God; Lord, hurry to my rescue."[83] In the Ethiopian tradition, the prayer was, "Jesus, have mercy on me! Jesus, help me! I praise you, my God!"[84] This was the beginning of the Jesus Prayer, an integral part of the mystical tradition of the Christian East. Today, the Jesus Prayer is the most widely used form of contemplative prayer in the world, the origins of which can be clearly traced to the experiences and writings of the Desert Fathers and Mothers.

The primary purpose of the Jesus Prayer is to deepen our relationship with him by encountering him in the stillness of the human heart. It is like listening at the feet of Jesus as Mary did. As Jesus told her sister Martha, who was overwhelmed with the chores of hospitality, Mary chose "the better portion."[85] This form of prayer can

---

80 *The Sayings of the Desert Fathers*, transl. Benedicta Ward, SLG (Kalamazoo, MI: Cistercian Publications, 1975), 131.

81 Luke 18:38.

82 Luke 18:13. See Parable of the Pharisee and Publican (Tax Collector), Luke 18:9-14.

83 Ps. 69:2.

84 See Bunge, *Earthen Vessels*, 120.

85 See Luke 10:38-42. For a discussion of the Mary-Martha dynamic, see A Deacon and Fellow Pilgrim, *Hearts Afire: Fulfilling Our Destiny* (Fairfax, VA: Eastern Christian Publications, 2014) 49-54. Conference No. 7. "First Things First."

help us set aside all earthly cares,[86] allowing our hearts to be lifted up to God.

The Work of Prayer

Desert Spirituality's silence and solitude creates an environment conducive to encounter. As St. Isaac the Syrian (640-700) wrote, "Silence is the sacrament of the world to come; words are the instrument of this present age."[87] Thus, the objective of hesychast prayer, as it evolved from Desert Spirituality, is interior stillness—a freeing from thoughts and other distractions, and an openness that creates an awareness of the presence of God.

In St. John Climacus's three-phase process, he cites a continuous desire to experience God in prayer. This type of "pure prayer" is a gift from God, granted to mystics who, in turn, experience a sense of union with him. As one modern spiritual elder from Mount Athos describes it:

> When God comes into our heart, he gains victory over the devil and cleanses the impurities which the evil one has created. The victory, therefore, over the devil is the victory of Christ in us. Let us do the human part by inviting Christ, and he will do the divine part by defeating the devil and purifying us.[88]

The elder also explained that the Jesus Prayer consists of two basic points of doctrine: acknowledges the divinity of Christ ("Lord Jesus Christ, Son of God") and confesses our inability to be saved through

---

86 Consider the words of the Cherubic Hymn in the Divine Liturgy of St. John Chrysostom, the predominate liturgy used in the Eastern Catholic and Orthodox Churches.

87 Quoted in John Breck, "Prayer of the Heart: Sacrament of the Presence of God," *Saint Vladimir's Theological Quarterly* 29(1) (1995), 26.

88 Metropolitan Hierotheos of Nafpaktos. *A Night in the Desert of the Holy Mountain: Discussion with a Hermit on the Jesus Prayer*, transl. Effie Mavromichali (Levadia, Greece: Birth of the Theotokos Monastery, 2009), 44.

our own merits ("Have mercy on me").[89] Jesus tells us that the Father in heaven already knows what we need before we ask.[90] Accordingly, all we truly need from God is his mercy. This acknowledges surrender of self-will to the Divine will ("Not my will but yours be done"[91]). The elder also explained: "We are not struggling to meet an impersonal God through the Jesus Prayer. We do not seek our elevation to absolute nothingness. Our prayer focuses on the personal God, the God-man Jesus."[92]

Over time and with continued practice, the individual will experience an insatiable thirst for the Jesus Prayer.[93] Yet, at the same time, virtually all Spiritual Fathers and Mothers will say that attaining true prayer is a struggle. We are under constant attacks by the demons that wish to steal our prayer and derail our relationship with God. These distractions are often referred to as *logismoi*—either positive or negative thoughts or impulses—which cause one to drift away from interior stillness and prayer.[94] Accordingly, we must remain persistent in our prayer, maintain our ardent desire, persevere in hope, retain our zeal, and exhibit immense patience, combined with faith in the love God has for us.[95] As St. Silouan the Athonite (1866-1938) advised:

> There is no comfortable armchair in the study for the monk to work out these problems. In the silence of the night, remote from the world, unheard and unseen,

---

89 Ibid., 45.

90 Cf. Matt. 6:8.

91 Luke 22:42. Also Matt. 26:39 and Mark 14:36. In John 6:38, Jesus states during his Bread of Life Discourse, "[B]ecause I came down from heaven not to do my own will but the will of the one who sent me." Throughout his ministry, Jesus models and describes the importance of complete obedience to the Father, so much so that it is included in the prayer he taught his disciples: "Your will be done on earth as in heaven" (Matt. 6:10).

92 Metropolitan Hierotheos of Nafpaktos, *A Night in the Desert of the Holy Mountain*, 50.

93 Ibid. See 170–171.

94 See A Deacon and Fellow Pilgrim. *Hearts Afire: A Personal Encounter with Jesus*, 2nd ed. (Fairfax, VA: Eastern Christian Publications, 2016), 34. Reference is made to *The Pilgrim's Tale*, in which attacks from the left are vain thoughts and sinful imaginings. Attacks from the right are edifying memories or beautiful thoughts. Both of these are distractions with one intent: to disrupt one's prayer and relationship with God.

95 Ibid., 81.

he falls down before God and weeps the prayer of the publican, "God be merciful to me, a sinner," or cries with St. Peter, "Lord, save me!"[96]

Elder Porphyrios, a monk who spent time on Mount Athos, advised:

Learn to love prayer. In order not to live in darkness, turn on the switch of prayer so that divine light may flood your soul. Christ will appear in the depths of your being. There, in the deepest and most inward part, is the Kingdom of God. The Kingdom of God is within you.[97]

Prayer nurtures our personal, intimate relationship with God, who asks that of us. It is a critical component to our vocation to holiness.

Cultivating Personal Prayer

St. Theophan the Recluse (1815-1894) wrote: "To pray means to stand before God with the mind, mentally to gaze unswervingly at him."[98] The key is to have the mind in the heart as we come before God. In theory, this makes sense; in practice, though, entering into contemplative prayer is quite challenging because it is very easy to become distracted. It is difficult to settle our thoughts, to achieve stillness, and to truly listen with our hearts. The demons and our sinfulness assail us. If we are experiencing separation or suffering or personal challenges, these distracting thoughts will encroach and make it more difficult to concentrate on God rather than ourselves (self-centeredness versus God-centeredness). As Abba Agathon (ca.

---

96   Sakharov, *St. Silouan the Athonite*, 166.
97   Elder Porphyrios, *Wounded by Love*, 113.
98   St. Theophan the Recluse. Taken from *The Art of Prayer*, comp. Igumen Chariton, transl. E. Kadloubovsky and G. E. H. Palmer (London: Farrar, Straus and Giroux, 1966), 17. Also from George Maloney, SJ. *Prayer of the Heart: The Contemplative Tradition of the Christian East* (Notre Dame, IN: Ave Maria Press, 2008), 65.

fourth century) said, prayer is the most difficult of work ("there is no labor greater than prayer"[99]); it requires great attention and practice to make progress in the spiritual life.

Abba Arsenius (ca. 350–445) provided three steps to personal prayer:

Flee/Withdraw Detach oneself from attachments and distractions. Seek a more authentic life rooted in God, reflecting that we are created in the divine image.

Silence Seek exterior and interior stillness. It is a freely-chosen willingness to let go of all that inhibits listening to God and knowing ourselves.[100]

Rest Find rest in the divine presence of God; gain refreshment from him. It is "an environment of grace when our hearts are expanded with the presence of God's energies and love. Inner peace gives birth to compassion because we have chosen to unite our desires with God's desires"[101] (surrender of self-will to the Divine will).

The Desert Fathers and Mothers believed the presence of God could be discovered in the heart. God fills the emptiness we create for him. The Desert Fathers and Mothers strove to pray and do as much of it as possible ("pray without ceasing") — all for the love of God, thereby moving into greater daily awareness of God's intimate and immediate loving presence. Increased awareness added by the Holy Spirit results in the gradual transformation of heart, gradually becoming more Christ-like, regaining the likeness of God — a conscious awareness of being one in Christ. This is *theosis*, the incremental awareness of God, gradually becoming more like him and preparing ourselves for our ultimate destiny, which is to share eternal blessedness with him.

---

99 *The Sayings of the Desert Fathers*, 22.
100 David G. R. Keller, *Oasis of Wisdom: The Worlds of the Desert Fathers and Mothers* (Collegeville, MN: Liturgical Press, 2005), 164.
101 Ibid.

As St. Paul wrote: "I live, no longer I, but Christ lives in me."[102]

Mary is the prime example for us, a wholly integrated person, totally surrendered in faith, and completely obedient to the will of God. She is the perfect human example of the surrender of self-will to the Divine will. "Behold, I am the handmaid of the Lord. May it be done to me according to your word."[103] Further, as stated in the Gospel, she "kept all these things, reflecting on them in her heart"[104] —an indication of contemplative life.

Contemplation is not about doing, but more about a state of being, an increased awareness of God's presence, and that our true selves are intrinsically tied to God. In the instructions of Abba Arsenius, contemplation is to be at rest (being, not doing). As St. Isaac the Syrian wrote, "The soul that loves God rests only in God."[105]

The Jesus Prayer: Placing Jesus at the Center of Our Lives

The Jesus Prayer is a simple, yet powerful tool for knowing the Lord Jesus in a very personal way in the silent recesses of our hearts. In effect, it places Jesus at the center of our lives. The following is an overview of the prayer itself:

---

102 Gal. 2:20. See also Maloney, *Prayer of the Heart*, 72.
103 Luke 1:38. This is often referred to as Mary's *fiat*, Latin for "Let it be done."
104 Luke 2:19.
105 *The Ascetical Homilies of Saint Isaac the Syrian*, rev. 2nd ed. (Boston: Holy Transfiguration Monastery, 2011), 141. Homily Four.

Breathing[106]	Prayer	Observation
Inhale	*Lord, Jesus Christ*[107]	**A profession of faith:**
Exhale	*Son of God*	Acknowledging Jesus as Lord, the center of our lives, and as the Son of God.
Inhale	*Have mercy on me*	**A desire for repentance and reconciliation:**
Exhale	*A sinner*	Acknowledging who we are ("a sinner") and our request of Jesus ("have mercy on me"). In addition, the prayer is grounded in humility—the foundation for attaining all the other virtues. Humility is part of the movement away from self, surrendering self-will to the divine will.

This prayer acknowledges a complete surrender to God, allowing Jesus to lead us on the spiritual journey to the Father. The Jesus Prayer is the only contemplative prayer tradition that approaches God with such a profound sense of humility. In today's world, there seems to be a loss of respect for God. This prayer focuses on the right-ordered relationship between Creator and creature, acknowledging the great difference between them and asking for the one thing we most need: *mercy*. We need not ask for anything more because Jesus tells us: "Your Father knows what you need before you ask him."[108] As one contemporary Athonite monk describes it, this is a prayer of the fallen

---

106 Some Spiritual Fathers would advise their disciples that the prayer is said on a single breath: (Inhale) "Lord Jesus Christ, Son of God"; (exhale) "have mercy on me, a sinner." Either means is acceptable, as long as the prayer itself becomes as natural as breathing. To some, this two-breath approach more readily adapts to a natural breathing pattern. Ultimately, it is up to the practitioner to decide what is better.

107 Acts 4:12: "There is no salvation through anyone else, nor is there any other *name* under heaven given to the human race by which we are to be saved."

108 Matt. 6:8.

person who acknowledges his or her sinfulness and, through the invocation of this prayer, asks God for divine mercy and light. "It is the language God loves to hear."[109]

It is important to note the Jesus Prayer is performed without mental forms or focusing on images, such as an icon. It is solely intended as a means to experience the presence of God. The breathing is meant to be natural, such that the prayer takes root in the heart, even when the practitioner is not conscious of it ("praying without ceasing"[110]).

Practicing the Jesus Prayer

The following is a practical discussion on how to pray the Jesus Prayer[111]:

1. **Posture** – Position your body comfortably, spine erect, using either a chair or cushions.

2. **Be Grounded** – Be aware of your physical senses. Close your eyes and gradually become aware of the physical senses of your body. Feel them as they flow through you.

3. **Open Your Awareness to God's Presence** – Feel the presence of God all around. Feel that presence within. Breathe in the Divine with every breath. Breathe God out, and let yourself rest in his presence. Begin slow, steady breathing with deep, natural breaths. Release outside thoughts and distractions.

4. **Move Thoughts from the Head to the Heart** – With every breath, allow the sphere of energy within to slowly sink from the head to the heart. This may be very difficult at first; slowly allow the energy within to become heavier and heavier, sinking to the heart one inch at a time. Center yourself in your

---

109 Monk Moses, *Athonite Flowers*, 41.
110 Cf. 1 Thess. 5:17.
111 The framework below leverages material from the following source: Ken Kaisch, *Finding God: A Handbook of Christian Meditation* (New York: Paulist Press, 1994), 199-200.

heart. This is why the Jesus Prayer is also referred to as "Prayer of the Heart."

5. **Begin the Words of the Prayer** – When a rhythm of breathing has been established, synchronize your breathing with the reverent repetition of the prayer. Slowly say the words from the heart: *"Lord, Jesus Christ, Son of God, have mercy on me, a sinner."* Let your heart repeat these words slowly, over and over again, feeling God's presence within. St. John Climacus writes: "The beginning of prayer is the expulsion of distractions from the very start by a single thought."[112] In this case, that single thought is the use of the Jesus Prayer.

6. **Be Attentive** – When your attention wanders, be patient. Thoughts and distractions are likely to emerge in one's consciousness during the Jesus Prayer (we can experience "Twitter-feed" in our minds, a constant bombardment of thoughts). Slowly refocus on the prayer, releasing the thoughts. "The goal is not to suppress the thoughts during prayer, but only to ignore them, to let them be and to let them go—and to *prefer* Jesus, to choose him anew whenever we wander."[113]

Fr. Thomas Keating, OCSO, (1923-2018) provided the best analogy for thoughts. He described human consciousness as a river and our thoughts as boats going down the river.[114] Suddenly in prayer, we realize that we are on one of these boats. Keating wrote: "If you find yourself on a boat, just get off. There should be no self-recriminations, no sighs, no annoyance that you had a thought. Any such reflection is another thought, another boat."[115]

112 St. John Climacus, *The Ladder of Divine Ascent*, 276. Step 28: "On Prayer." The Greek term used for thought, *monologistōs*, can also mean "by a repeated short prayer."
113 Joseph Langford, MC, *Mother Teresa's Secret Fire* (Huntington, IN: Our Sunday Visitor, 2008), 196.
114 See Thomas Keating, *Intimacy with God* (New York: The Crossroad Publishing Company, 2002), 61-63.
115 Ibid., 63.

We should not judge ourselves for having a thought. Just gently let it go and return to the prayer. Remember the intention: to enter into prayer, to cultivate the relationship with God. God is more interested in our intention than whether we do the prayer perfectly, which we cannot. Gently we bring ourselves back to attentiveness (head in the heart, rhythmically breathing, and the slow repetition of the prayer: *Lord, Jesus Christ, Son of God, have mercy on me, a sinner*).

Consider the Four "R's" related to interior stillness:

- Do not **Resist** the thought. We are human beings; rational thought is part of who we are. It was a gift from our Creator.

- Do not **Retain** the thought. Once you realize your mind has wandered, gently let go of the thought. If you find yourself on a boat, simply get off.

- Gently **Return** to the prayer.

- Do not **Regret** the thought. The purpose of the prayer is intention—to build a relationship with the unseen God, who knows this intention. Regret is another thought, another boat going down the river. Regret is also a demon that can result in despair and discouragement, preventing us from continuing our prayer.

The repetition of the prayer is not a monotonous attempt to gain God's attention,[116] essentially trying to wear down God, but an attempt to change oneself by clearing one's mind of everything except Jesus. The goal is to make this prayer so connected with one's breathing that it becomes, as the experienced Fathers say, truly rooted in our hearts and continues as unconscious or self-activating prayer.

---

116 Cf. Matt. 6:7.

Regarding distractions (*logismoi*), the "enemy" who despises prayer will do *anything* to disrupt our efforts. Assaults come from the left ("vain thoughts and sinful imaginings"[117]) and from the right ("edifying memories" or "beautiful thoughts"[118]). All such thoughts are meant to disrupt us from our prayer. Keep in mind what is important to God. He is pleased when we persevere in our prayer, that we stay the course no matter how intense the distractions.

7. **Conclude the Jesus Prayer** – When you are ready, let the feeling return to your hands, feet, and face. Take a deep breath and slowly open your eyes. This prayer was intended for a monastic to perform in his or her cell. Accordingly, each person chooses when to conclude his or her prayer. The prayer is not about completing a specified number of repetitions. What is most important is to simply spend time in silence with Jesus.

8. **Use a Prayer Rope** – Eastern Catholic monastics often use a prayer rope to count the number of recitations of the Jesus Prayer. It also helps one remain focused on the prayer. Tradition has it that St. Pachomius (292-348), an Egyptian and early Desert Father, invented the prayer rope as an aid for illiterate monks to accomplish a consistent number of prayers and prostrations in their cells. Prayer ropes come in varying lengths; however, ropes with 100 beads (usually with a knotted cross on the end) and 33 beads are the most common.

---

117 *The Pilgrim's Tale*, transl. T. Allan Smith (New York/Mahwah: Paulist Press, 1999), 108.
118 Ibid.

The Jesus Prayer is meant to be very personal, done in private to reflect the instructions of Jesus in Matt. 6:6 ("Enter the inner room, close the door, and pray to your Father in secret").

Jesus Prayer Practicum

St. Isaac the Syrian tells us we cannot taste honey by reading a book.[119] God is not meant to be intellectualized; he is meant to be experienced. Similarly, we can discuss the history and merits of the Jesus Prayer; however, it is important for us to experience the prayer: to taste its sweetness, and be sustained by its fruits. Take some time to pause, to be still, and to enter into the Jesus Prayer.

Allow retreat participants to enter into prayer for 15-20 minutes. Once the time has passed, gently bring them back. Then ask the following question for a short group discussion.

Group Discussion Question:

Would anyone like to describe his or her experience with the Jesus Prayer?

---

119 See *The Ascetical Homilies of Saint Isaac the Syrian*, 153. Homily Four. "Therefore, O man, pay attention to what you read here. Indeed, can these things be known from [*writings of*] ink? Or can the taste of honey pass over the palate by reading books? For if you do not strive, you will not find, and if you do not knock at the door with vehemence and keep constant vigil before it, you will not be heard."

The Fruit of Prayer

Previously, we spoke of the "work" of prayer. Like any skill, it requires practice and persistence, which will result in the fruit—a deeper faith and relationship with Christ. That is why we are advised to have a Rule of Prayer, setting aside time each day, preferably at the same time, to spend with the Lord. As Matthew Kelly writes, "We learn to live deeply by praying deeply. Make your prayer time a sacred item on your schedule. Make it non-negotiable. Strong daily routines are life-giving, and prayer is the first of them."[120]

The fruit of prayer is a gift granted by God in response to our work. "The quality and intensity of prayer that leads to abiding communion with God are bestowed only by the Spirit."[121] The cultural challenge for us in a 5G world is not seeing instant results from our efforts. As a current-day Athonite monk writes:

> A characteristic of contemporary man, who is easy-going in some ways, is a strong sense of hurry, and great impatience. He expects a great deal quickly and without much toil. The impatience which possesses him makes him want to hurry in prayer; he wants instant results, here and now. He wants to reap the fruit before even sowing. Without a drop of sweat, he expects miracles, visions, and revelations.[122]

We cannot force or manipulate prayer. Like any regimen, we must simply persevere at the work. As advised in the famous spiritual classic *Unseen Warfare*:

---

120 Matthew Kelly, *Rediscover the Saints*, 33.
121 Breck, "Prayer of the Heart: Sacrament of the Presence of God," 38. Consider Rom. 8:26: "For we do not know how to pray as we ought, but the Spirit itself intercedes with inexpressible groanings." This verse supports the concept of *synergeia*, human and divine collaboration.
122 Monk Moses, *Athonite Flowers*, 70.

> Do not set a time for achievement in this prayer. Decide only one thing: to work, and to work. Months and years will go by before the first feeble indications of success begin to show. One of the Mount Athos fathers said of himself that two years of work passed before his heart grew warm. With another father this warmth came after eight months. With each man it comes in accordance with his powers and his diligence in the work.[123]

The true art of prayer is taught by God himself to the person who prays. Through joy and inner peace, he will inform us if our prayer is true and pleasing to him.[124]

Conclusion

In this conference we discussed the importance of prayer, one component of the interior life. As Cardinal Sarah writes, "Faith grows in an intense life of prayer and contemplative silence."[125] However, the other components cannot be neglected because they nourish our faith.[126] This includes the sacramental life of the Church, in particular the Holy Mysteries of Repentance (Confession) and Holy Eucharist. These are considered roots for a life of prayer.[127] Sacred Scripture is also important: "For one who desires to live the life of prayer, daily nourishment from Sacred Scripture is indispensable. Study of the Bible expedites the intervention of God in our lives."[128] Together with prayer, these represent the fullness of the interior spiritual life.

---

123 *Unseen Warfare: Being the Spiritual Combat and Path to Paradise of Lorenzo Scupoli*, ed. Nicodemus of the Holy Mountain, rev. Theophan the Recluse, transl. E. Kadloubovsky and G. E. H. Palmer (London: Faber and Faber, 1963), 161.

124 See Monk Moses, *Athonite Flowers*, 74.

125 Robert Cardinal Sarah, *The Day is Now Far Spent*, 26,

126 Ibid. Cardinal Sarah writes: "Faith is nourished by the liturgy, Catholic doctrine, and by the Church's tradition as a whole. Its principal sources are Sacred Scripture, the Fathers of the Church, and the Magisterium."

127 Ibid., 63.

128 Ibid., 61.

In creating the right atmosphere for our prayer, to truly cultivate the interior life, we should be frequent participants in the Holy Mysteries, read Sacred Scripture, and adopt some of the ascetical practices such as fasting, which are discussed in the next conference. These in combination represent the Art of Spiritual Life.

Movie

It is highly recommended for participants to watch at least the first part of the following film, up to and including the visit to St. Antony's Monastery in Egypt (~13 minutes).

Mysteries of the Jesus Prayer. Norris Chumley and Rev. Dr. John A. McGuckin, 2011.

Reflection Questions

1. How would I describe my prayer life today? What is my personal Rule of Prayer? Is contemplative prayer part of this?

2. Would I consider myself as having a personal relationship with Jesus, wherein I encounter him in prayer and recognize his presence in different points in my life? Please explain and please be honest.

3. What specifically holds me back from a deeper relationship with God? Am I simply too busy for a relationship?

4. Do I desire a deeper relationship with God? If yes, what am I willing to do to build this relationship? If no, is there a reason that a relationship with God is not sufficiently important to me?

Icon of the Transfiguration.

"Jesus took Peter, John, and James and went up to the mountain to pray" (Luke 9:28). At the Transfiguration, these apostles experienced an encounter with the divinity of Christ. The purpose of this encounter was to provide a foretaste of eternal blessedness, a reminder to strengthen them for the events that would lay ahead in Jerusalem (the passion, death, and resurrection). Accordingly, in most works on *theosis*, the predominant cover image is an icon of the Transfiguration.

CONFERENCE NO. 3

Formation

"For where your treasure is, there also will your heart be."
(Matt. 6:21)

"The simpler, better, and more loving a person is, the more blessed he is inwardly; the more deceitful, evil, and selfish he is, the more unhappy."[129]
(St. John of Kronstadt)

"The Christian religion transforms people and heals them. The most important precondition, however, for someone to recognize and discern the truth is humility."
(Elder Porphyrios)

Introduction to the Conference

In our opening conference, we introduced the concept of a vocation to holiness. Jesus asks of us, "Be with me. Let me lead you, guide you, teach you. Let me give you strength. Surrender yourself to me and I will take care of everything." In the second conference, we discussed developing a personal relationship with Jesus Christ through encounter, with a specific focus on prayer. Like the apostles, we also want to be formed by Jesus, because from Sacred Scripture we see how that formation bore abundant fruit once they received the Holy Spirit at Pentecost.

In addition to encountering Jesus through prayer and the sacramental life of the Church, we can reflect on his teachings and actions within the Gospel. Jesus had a threefold ministry: "He preached the Good News; he built up the community of believers;

---

129 St. John of Kronstadt, *My Life in Christ*, Part 1, 91.

and he served those around him, especially those in need."[130] This becomes our foundation, just as it was for the apostles. Then, we can consider how this formed faith was practiced by the apostles (Acts of the Apostles), how it was further interpreted through the Epistles, and then we can also see how the faith was lived through the lives and writings of the Church Fathers and Mothers. Thus, the teachings and life of Jesus become an important foundation for our formation, through which we become the disciples who continue to build up the Church and the Kingdom here on earth.

Fair warning: The teachings of Jesus were radical departures from the common conventions of his day and, similarly, are significant departures from the messages and promises we hear in our secular society. However, only Christ is the source of life, and to remain with him, to be formed by him, means to follow him and imitate the examples he left us.

Opening Gospel Passage

Read: Matt. 6:19-34 (Dependence on God).

Putting the Teachings of Jesus into Context

Jesus was not who the people expected him to be; maybe he wasn't even who they wanted him to be. They had preconceived notions of the *messiah*, in contrast with the reality of the mission and purpose Jesus proclaimed. We, too, can be led astray by our preconceived notions of Jesus rather than who he truly is. We cannot form Jesus (or God) into our image of what we want him to be. Rather, it is we who are created in the divine image.

At the time of Jesus, the *messiah* was anticipated to be the person who was to liberate Israel and restore the kingdom of David. Because

---

130 Chaput, *Living the Catholic Faith*, 71.

Palestine was occupied by the Romans, it was anticipated this person would be a king or general or great conqueror—someone powerful enough to end Roman rule. Yet the liberation Jesus proclaimed was the forgiveness of sins. At the beginning of his ministry, he went to the synagogue in Nazareth and read from the scroll from the Prophet Isaiah that he came to bring glad tidings to the poor and liberty to captives.[131] Most people then were poor and considered sinners by the religious authorities. In fact, when the temple guards failed to arrest Jesus because of the crowds and their amazement at his teaching, the chief priests retorted, "Have you also been deceived? Have any of the authorities or the Pharisees believed in him? But this crowd, which does not know the law, is accursed."[132] Essentially, they were written off by the Sadducees (priestly class) and Pharisees.

> To forgive someone is to liberate them from the domination of their past. Jesus's gesture of friendship (to the outcast) made it quite clear that this was precisely what he had in mind. He overlooked their past and refused to hold anything at all against them. He treated them as people who were no longer, if ever, indebted to God and therefore no longer deserving of rejection and punishment. They were forgiven.[133]

Jesus turned the teachings of his day upside down and liberated people from their sins, from the belief bestowed upon them by the religious authorities that they were unworthy, and restored their dignity in the eyes of God. He deliberately sought out and befriended tax collectors, prostitutes, those caught in adultery or inappropriate relationships (e.g., the Samaritan woman at the well), the blind, the lame, and the leper. Although they were despised and rejected by the religious authorities ("accursed"), Jesus's actions showed them they

---

131 See Luke 4:16-21.
132 John 7:48-49. Another translation says, "But this mob that does not know the Law—they're under a curse!" (International Standard Version).
133 Albert Nolan, *Jesus Before Christianity* (Maryknoll, NY: Orbis Books, 2013), 48-49.

were loved by their Heavenly Father. This was not the liberation most people had in mind.

"In the society in which Jesus lived, money was the second most important value. The dominant value was *prestige*."[134] Many likely thought the *messiah* would be someone of prestige. Yet Jesus said, "Whoever wishes to be great among you (prestige) shall be your servant (humility); whoever wishes to be first among you shall be your slave."[135] He taught, "Amen, I say to you, whoever does not accept the kingdom of God like a child (vulnerable) will not enter it."[136] When he entered Jerusalem, Jesus was not seated upon a magnificent horse, but on a donkey—a beast of service. At the Last Supper, Jesus washed the feet of his disciples[137] —an ultimate act of humility generally performed by a slave. He told his disciples, "I have given you a model to follow, so that as I have done for you, you should also do."[138]

Wealth was considered a reward from God for virtuous living (rich = virtuous; poor = sinner). Yet Jesus taught, "Blessed are the poor in spirit, for theirs is the kingdom of heaven."[139] He advised the crowds, "Do not store up for yourselves treasures on earth … but store up treasures in heaven."[140] When the rich young man went away sad, Jesus noted, "Amen, I say to you, it will be hard for one who is rich to enter the kingdom of heaven."[141] He warned about the dangers of wealth and focusing solely on one's self, as in the Parable of the Rich Fool.[142] Again, Jesus turned upside down the social conventions of his time.

At the Presentation of Jesus in the temple, Simeon had made this prediction to his mother, Mary: "Behold, this child is destined for the fall

---

134 Ibid., 67.
135 Matt. 20:26.
136 Mark 10:15. The most vulnerable of society, the *anawim*, were the widow the orphan, and the resident alien. They had no voice in society.
137 See John 13:1-15.
138 John 13:15.
139 Matt. 5:3.
140 Matt. 6:19-20.
141 Matt. 19:23.
142 Luke 12:13-21.

and rise of many in Israel, and to be a sign that will be contradicted."[143] In Gospel accounts, we see this played out. The religious authorities (scribes, Pharisees, Sadducees) — those considered the righteous at the time—rejected the teaching of Jesus and the kingdom of heaven (the fall). Those who were outcasts and sinners were restored to friendship with God (the rise). In fact, in the Gospel of Luke, the tax collectors and sinners often were shown drawing near to Jesus to listen to the word of God, in contrast to the Pharisees, who were generally criticizing and rejecting these teachings, fiercely clinging to the status quo.[144] However, as Jesus said at the repentance of Zacchaeus, "The Son of Man has come to seek and to save what was lost."[145] This was the ultimate liberation, freeing those bearing heavy burdens placed upon them by the scribes and Pharisees, and being reliant on these authorities for their well-being.[146]

Jesus essentially changed the view of riches, honor, and pride, which were the three temptations he experienced in the desert. Rather, he recommended that his followers embrace spiritual poverty and endure insults and contempt, from which would come genuine humility.[147] This was extremely radical, and we can imagine the crowds murmuring, "This teaching is hard; who can accept it?"[148]

Are we any more able to accept this teaching today?

Becoming More God-like

Our objective is to become more like God, preparing ourselves to share in eternal blessedness with him. First, this involves a decision to surrender our own will to God's will, moving from self-centeredness

---

143 Luke 2:34.
144 See for example Luke 15:1-2.
145 Luke 19:10.
146 See Matt. 23:3-4. "For they preach and do not practice. They tie up heavy burdens [hard to carry] and lay them on people's shoulders, but will not lift a finger to move them."
147 See William A. Barry, SJ, Finding God in All Things (Notre Dame, IN: Ave Maria Press, 1991), 102-103.
148 John 6:60.

to God-centeredness. We become reliant on God in our obedience to him. Second, the incremental transformation we experience (*theosis*) means we will gradually begin to exhibit the attributes of God. We can look to the example of Jesus and his teachings to determine some of those attributes: goodness, love, mercy, compassion, longsuffering,[149] patience, purity, and having pure love for neighbor.[150] To become whom God wants us to be and to fulfill our destiny of eternal blessedness with him, we too must follow the example of Jesus, allowing him to form us and further develop these attributes. We begin by considering Jesus's definition of discipleship: "If anyone wishes to come after me, he must deny himself and take up his cross daily and follow me."[151] That means a life of self-denial, bearing hardships, and cultivating virtue. "The way for the Christian is crucifixion."[152] The good news is that we know the way. However, sometimes the immensity of the task seems overwhelming.[153]

Like an Olympic athlete, we must constantly train ourselves and remain focused to achieve our goal. The spiritual disciplines include the practice of the virtues, beginning with humility, ascetical practices such as fasting and self-denial (*áskēsis*), detachment from disordered passions such as material possessions (*apatheia*), mourning of our own sinfulness (compunction or *penthos*), sober vigilance (*nepsis*), and forgiveness of others (*aphesei*), just to name a few. This requires time and effort. Further, our prayer must be in harmony with our lives. We cannot live reckless or careless lives and expect to achieve a fruitful prayer relationship with God. We must create the right environment.

Consider the wisdom of St. Isaac the Syrian: "The fear of God is the beginning of virtue, and it is said to be the offspring of faith.

---

149 Longsuffering is more than simply perseverance. By definition, longsuffering means "long and patient endurance of injury, trouble, or provocation." We consider the example of Jesus, his extreme humility and self-surrender, especially during his passion.

150 The divine attributes or what God wants us to become can be seen through Jesus's life in the Gospels. Taken from A Monk of Mount Athos, *The Watchful Mind: Teachings on the Prayer of the Heart*, transl. George Dokos (Yonkers, NY: St. Vladimir's Seminary Press, 2014), 160.

151 Luke 9:23.

152 Sakharov, *We Shall See Him As He Is*, 70.

153 Ibid.

It is sown in the heart when a man withdraws his mind from the attractions of the world."[154] Fear in this sense means "reverential fear" and awe at the majesty of God. It is an acknowledgment of the great difference between Creator and created, whereby we recognize and approach God with a profound sense of humility, knowing that he in all his glory desires a personal relationship with us. Thus, this fear of God, this profound sense of awe and humility, reflects a heart that begins to be conditioned to practice the virtues. It is a transformed heart, not one of a superficial or intellectualized faith. Consider again the example of Zacchaeus. When he welcomes Jesus into his home, Zacchaeus acknowledges his past of defrauding others and wants to make restitution. Further, he offers to give half of his wealth to the poor. This reflects a true, interior change of heart (*metanoia*).

Asceticism

To Jesus, discipleship includes denial of self, or turning away from the "world" through ascetical practices. How can we do that today? Our life of "convenience" has actually become quite complicated. In contrast, the Early Desert Fathers and Mothers[155] sought a life of simplicity, freeing themselves of attachments and coming to a realization that what people often valued in secular society really had no value.[156] Their approach was following Jesus's commandment to the fullest: "Sell all that you have and distribute it to the poor, and you will have a treasure in heaven. Then come, follow me."[157] Often we think our attachments will bring us happiness. However, only complete dependence on God and allowing his plan for our lives to unfold can bring us true happiness.

---

154 *The Ascetical Homilies of Saint Isaac the Syrian*, 113. Homily One.
155 We like the example of the Desert Fathers and Mothers from the Early Church (third to eighth centuries) because it represents a back-to-basics spirituality: authentic, organic, no additives or preservatives. Further, this Desert Spirituality underpins the mystical tradition of the Christian East, having been faithfully practiced and preserved since post-Apostolic times.
156 See also Phil 3:7-8.
157 Luke 18:22.

Ascetical practices are appropriate for people from all walks of life, not just monastics. A number of spiritual writers speak about a sense of "interior monasticism" to describe a condition of simplicity that all disciples of Jesus can follow. It is not necessarily about severity or "checking the box"; rather, it is the genuine practice of self-denial as described by Jesus to strengthen our relationship by being dependent on our loving Father. In a world poverty-stricken for an appreciation of true love, we practice spiritual poverty to achieve what Jesus taught: "Blessed are the poor in spirit, for the kingdom of heaven is theirs."[158] We also practice spiritual poverty to avoid self-centeredness and loss of connection with our neighbor.

Our attachments often come through habits or practices—and we may not realize how many we have. Often, these are subconscious pursuits of happiness and/or a focus on self. Consider these questions: What attachments do I have? Why do I have them? What is necessary or sufficient, and what is extra?

- Retail therapy (*Just imagine what this term implies!*).

- Designer clothes / attachment to particular brands.

- The latest technology or video games.

- Collections: books, CDs, stereo equipment, clothes, purses, shoes.

- Daily routines: workouts, daily Starbucks stop, surfing the Internet.

- Life revolving around certain television programs or other forms of entertainment.

- Exotic trips or vacations.

- Other? — Let's face it, we all have them.

In our culture today, "acquisition seems to be synonymous with happiness. This snare becomes a form of slavery, bringing jealousy and

---

158 Matt. 5:3.

hatred with it."[159] "Television the Internet, and many other communication technologies monopolize the time that is meant for God."[160]

How can I simplify my life?

- Eat simplified meals certain days per week; try fasting or meatless Wednesdays and Fridays, even outside the Great Fast, following the Church's cycle of fasts.

- Plan weekly meals at home with family.

- Reprioritize where and how I spend my time.

- Spend a day without television or the Internet, earbuds, or headphones.

- Eliminate the attraction to brands and designer labels—we are not what we own or wear.

- Remove other attachments (denial of self).

- Perform other ascetical practices and acts of self-denial.

In a culture in which consumption has become so prevalent, where we want things here and now, we run the risk of becoming enslaved consumers and our interior lives can begin to atrophy.[161] We can find ourselves spiritually exhausted. The goal of simplification is the purification of our lives through self-denial, the liberation of our souls and bodies from sin and attachments, the reprioritization of our lives, the strengthening of our relationship with Christ ("follow me"), and increasing our capacity to love our neighbor. Further, as Jesus taught: "Blessed are the clean (pure) of heart, for they will see God."[162] Accordingly, we can be more attuned to the presence of God in our lives when surrounded by less distractions. As Cardinal Sarah

---

159 Robert Cardinal Sarah, *The Day is Now Far Spent*, 238.
160 Ibid., 234.
161 See Ibid., 237.
162 Matt. 5:8.

advises, "We urgently need to rediscover the meaning of authentic Christian asceticism."[163]

To be sure, attachments alone do not necessarily cause us to sin. However, they can dull our senses in terms of our priorities, thus diminishing our reliance upon God and our ability to trust him as the giver of all blessings. Attachments can cause us to be complacent and to lose focus.

St. John of Kronstadt invites us to self-examination, having written:

> That which a man loves, to which he inclines, that he will find. If he loves the worldly, he will find the worldly, and it will settle in his heart, making him earthly and binding him. If he loves the heavenly, he will find the heavenly, and it will settle in his heart and give him life.[164]

> Examine yourself more; where are the eyes of your heart directed? Are they turned toward God and the life to come, toward the most peaceful, blessed, resplendent, heavenly, holy powers dwelling in heaven? Or are they turned toward the world, toward earthly blessings—to food, drink, dress, house, to sinful men and their vain occupations? If only the eyes of your heart were always fixed on God![165]

Detachment is a way of renouncing our excess baggage. The plain, simple truth is this: "We can always manage with less than we have; indeed, we often can manage with a lot less than we would dare to imagine."[166] Some have had to learn this lesson because of an economic downturn, loss of employment, illness, or other crises.

---

163 Robert Cardinal Sarah, *The Day is Now Far Spent*, 236.
164 St. John of Kronstadt, *My Life in Christ*, Part 1, 66.
165 Ibid.
166 John Chryssavgis, *In the Heart of the Desert: The Spirituality of the Desert Fathers and Mothers* (Bloomington, IN: World Wisdom, Inc., 2003), 83.

However, such experiences are gifts from God because he alone knows best what we need. As Dorotheos of Gaza (c. 505-565) wrote: "Above all let us be convinced that nothing can happen to us apart from the providence of God."[167] This is the life Jesus modeled for us and asks us to embrace as his disciples.

Surrender of Self-Will to the Divine Will

One of Jesus's greatest acts of humility is his surrender to the will of the Father, modeled both in the Garden of Gethsemane ("Not as I will, but as you will"[168]) and surrendering all to his Father on the cross ("Father, into your hands I commend my spirit"[169]). To remain in Christ and to prepare ourselves for eternal blessedness, sharing in the Life of the Holy Trinity, we need to completely align our will with the Divine will. This surrender is also extremely difficult, one of the greatest challenges we face. Our egos resist letting go of control, thus standing in the way of what God desires for us.[170] Further, we live in a culture of individualism (self over others), where the person is the center instead of God and emphasis is placed on our own abilities, personal success, and instant material happiness.[171]

Individualism is more than simple selfishness; it is innate to our culture, which has evolved as the importance of God began to be diminished. Accordingly, behaviors of today, such as "looking out for number one," are considered normal.[172] Many do not even realize or appreciate how the culture has impacted their views on faith, such as love of God and love of neighbor.

---

167 Dorotheos of Gaza, *Discourses and Sayings*, transl. Eric P. Wheeler (Kalamazoo, MI: Cistercian Publications, 1977), 143. Discourse VII, "On Self-accusation."

168 Matt. 26:39.

169 Luke 23:46.

170 See David G. R. Keller, *Desert Banquet: A Year of Wisdom from the Desert Mothers and Fathers* (Collegeville, MN: Liturgical Press, 2011), 140.

171 Cf. Robert Cardinal Sarah, "You follow me," *Magnificat*, 19/4 (2017), 54.

172 "Culture of Individualism" is a term coined by Archbishop Charles J. Chaput of Philadelphia in his book *Strangers in a Strange Land: Practicing the Catholic Faith in a Post-Christian World* (New York: Henry Holt, 2017).

If removed from the center of our lives, God becomes distant, less relevant, and the importance of Christian values is reduced. As written in the Second Letter of John, "Anyone who is so 'progressive' as not to remain in the teaching of Christ does not have God; whoever remains in the teaching has the Father and the Son."[173] Remember, Christ is the only true source of life. Separation from God is torment, despair, and death. Accordingly, in pursuing our vocation to holiness, we cannot succumb to the promises and hype of the secular world, or become complacent in our spiritual journey. There is either life in Christ or darkness. There is no middle way.[174] It is all too easy to fall in with the environment surrounding us because the vocation to holiness is increasingly the path less traveled and increasingly at odds with the secular world.[175]

Humility is the Foundation of the Virtues

St. Gregory of Nyssa describes the spiritual journey and how humility is the keystone from which the other virtues flow. If one virtue exists, the others are believed to exist as well because the virtues are indivisible.[176] To be humble, we also need to reflect on Jesus, who is humility personified, and the self-emptying love by which he gave himself to others. We begin with his self-emptying through the Incarnation (kenosis) in order to take on our humanity,[177] his humble birth, his model of humility at the Last Supper by washing the feet of his disciples, and his complete surrender to his Heavenly Father in

---

173 2 John 9.
174 See Rev. 3:15-16. Warning to the Church in Laodicea: "I know your works; I know that you are neither cold nor hot. I wish you were either cold or hot. So, because you are luke-warm, neither hot nor cold, I will spit you out of my mouth."
175 See John 16:33. "In the world, you will have trouble, but take courage, I have conquered the world."
176 St. Gregory of Nyssa, "On the Beatitudes," in Ancient Christian Writers: The Works of the Fathers in Translation, vol. 18, ed. Johannes Quasten and Joseph C. Plumpe, transl. Hilda C. Graef (New York: Paulist Press, 1954), 125. Sermon 4: "For any one form of virtue, divorced from the others, could never by itself be a perfect virtue."
177 See Phil. 2:7. "He emptied himself, taking the form of a slave, coming in human likeness; and found human in appearance."

his passion and crucifixion.[178] As Jesus said, "Whoever wishes to be first among you shall be your slave."[179] This was a clear message in his teaching, and Jesus modeled this by his life.

If humility creates a state of peace and it cannot be divorced from the other virtues, then developing a life of virtue contributes to a fitting interior environment for encounter. As St. Silouan the Athonite advised his disciple, "Therefore I tell you, humble yourself at all times, and be content with the gifts you are given, and then you will be living with God."[180] St. John of Kronstadt advises us:

> Humble yourself, consider yourself as nothing but grass, which is insignificant compared to ancient oak trees, or as a prickly thorn, which is worthless compared to fragrant flowers. You are indeed grass; you are indeed a prickly thorn because of your passions.[181]

Passions and temptations will be discussed further below.

Jesus is Our Model for Humility

In our vocation to holiness, we need to follow Jesus's example. He must be our guide, to fill our hearts and slowly replace the pride, self-centeredness, jealousy, pettiness, anger, judgments, covetousness, carnal desires, and all the other filth we have within. Elder Porphyrios advised that for Christ to love us, he must discover something special in us: humility.[182] Without it, the divine grace we need to achieve our vocation to holiness will not enter our hearts. We cannot undergo this transformation alone; we depend on Jesus to guide and assist us. As

---

178 See Phil. 2:8. "He humbled himself, becoming obedient to death, even death on a cross."
179 Matt. 20:27.
180 Sakharov, *St. Silouan the Athonite*, 169.
181 St. John of Kronstadt, *My Life in Christ*, Part 2, transl. E. E. Goulaeff. Revised and adapted by Nicholas Kotar (Jordanville, NY: Holy Trinity Monastery, 2015), 81.
182 Elder Porphyrios, *Wounded by Love*, 109.

Choosing Life in Christ

Jesus tells us, "Learn from me for I am meek and humble of heart."[183]

Consider the following:

- Jesus embraced poverty:

    - Jesus entered the world without attachments: He did not have his own bed (he had a manger) or clothes (he was wrapped in swaddling clothes).[184] Despite our romanticized view of the Christmas story, swaddling clothes were scraps of cloth or dirty rags.

    - Jesus left this world without attachments, stripped of his garments at the foot of the cross.[185]

- Jesus experienced temptation[186] — temptations that are similar to what we as human beings experience, most revolving around pleasure (bread represents giving into self-desire, food, drink, or lust), self-importance/recognition ("throw yourself down" is putting the Lord our God to the test), and power ("all the kingdoms of the world in their magnificence").

- Jesus fed the hungry, attending to their basic needs in the multiplication of loaves and fish before teaching the people.[187]

- Jesus healed the blind,[188] the lame,[189] and the deaf;[190] he cleansed the leper[191] and he drove out demons.[192] These were the people labeled as "sinners" by the social conventions of the time and were shunned. Jesus restored their dignity as sons and daughters of God.

---

183 See Matt. 11:29.
184 See Luke 2:7.
185 See Matt. 27:35, Mark 15:21, Luke 23:24, and John 19:23.
186 See Matt. 4:1-11.
187 See Matt. 14:14-20, Mark 6:35-44, Luke 9:12-17, and John 6:5-13.
188 See Matt. 9:27, 12:22, 20:30, Mark 8:22, 10:46, Luke 18:35, John 5:3, John 9:1.
189 See Matt. 15:20.
190 See Mark 7:32 and 9:25.
191 See Matt 8:2, Mark 1:40, and Luke 17:12
192 See Matt. 8:16, 8:28, 9:32, 12:22, 17:14, Mark 1:32, 1:34, 1:39, 5:2, Luke 4:33, 4:41, 8:27, 9:37, and 11:14.

- Jesus showed compassion, such as to the woman caught in the act of adultery[193] and the Samaritan woman at the well.[194]

- Jesus embraced the outcasts and the outsiders, such as the blind man on the road to Jericho,[195] Zacchaeus the tax collector,[196] the Syrophoenician woman who requested healing for her daughter,[197] and the Roman centurion who wished his serving boy to be healed.[198]

- Jesus demonstrated humility, performing the task of a slave when washing the feet of his disciples.[199]

- Jesus suffered rejection, in both his hometown of Nazareth[200] and in Jerusalem.[201]

- Jesus surrendered to the Will of His Father— "Not my will, but yours."[202]

- Jesus was silent when he was humiliated. He opened not his mouth when he was scourged, insulted, slapped, spat upon, crowned with thorns, and stripped of his garments before the crowds.[203]

- Jesus forgave his persecutors: "Forgive them, Father, for they know not what they do."[204]

- Jesus took care of his followers at the foot of the cross. He

---

193 See John 8:3-11.
194 See John 4:7-42.
195 See Mark 10:46-52 and Luke 18:35-43.
196 See Luke 19:2-10.
197 See Mark 15:22-28.
198 See Matt. 8:5-13 and Luke 7:2-10.
199 See John 13:4-15.
200 See Matt. 13:54-58 and Mark 6:2-6.
201 See Matt. 27:22, Mark 15:23, Luke 23:21, and John 19:6.
202 Luke 22:42.
203 See Is. 53:7. "Though harshly treated, he submitted and did not open his mouth; like a lamb led to the slaughter or a sheep silent before shearers, he did not open his mouth." Isaiah Chapter 53 is a foretelling of the passion narrative.
204 Luke 23:34.

entrusted the care of his mother to the beloved disciple and he gave the beloved disciple a mother.[205]

• Jesus trusted His Father implicitly— "Father, into your hands I commend my spirit."[206]

• Jesus offered his life on the cross for our redemption.[207]

Jesus is indeed our model for humility as well as detachment from material goods (wealth), glory (prestige), and pride. As he tells us: "If anyone wishes to come after me, he must deny himself and take up his cross daily and follow me."[208] He also says, "Whoever does not carry his own cross and come after me cannot be my disciple."[209] Thus, there is no ambiguity as to what is required in terms of discipleship. Accordingly, in our vocation to holiness, the teachings of Jesus coupled with his example become part of our formation, if we desire to become *authentic* Christian disciples.

Overcoming Passions and Temptations

The Spiritual Fathers and Mothers speak of the need to overcome the passions or appetites that often drive human behavior. Pride is the first of these passions to be overcome through the cultivation of humility, since this is the foundational virtue.[210] In order to create the right conditions for prayer and vigilance, we need to overcome our passions by channeling these energies toward God. Consider the following[211]:

---

205 See John 19:26-27.
206 Luke 23:46.
207 See John 19:30.
208 Luke 9:23.
209 Luke 14:27.
210 See *The Ascetical Homilies of Saint Isaac the Syrian*, 113. Homily One. "The fear of God is the beginning of virtue." In this context, fear of God is the prerequisite and humility is the foundational virtue upon which all the other virtues are built.
211 See Kallistos Ware, *The Philokalia: Master Reference Guide*, comp. Basileios S. Stapkis, ed. Gerald Eustace Howell Palmer and Philip Sherrard (Minneapolis: Light & Life Publishing Company, 2004), xiv. Author added "Ingratitude/Indifference" to the list.

Passion to be conquered	By being transformed into
Pride	Humility
Lust	*Agapé* love
Anger	Righteous indignation (emotional response to injustice, mistreatment, insult, malice)
Greed	Selfless love and generosity; detachment from material possessions and wants
Unfaithfulness	Fidelity; firm resolution; unwavering
Envy	Magnanimity (generous in forgiving insults or injury; free from petty resentments or vindictiveness)
Sloth	Diligence and zeal
Ingratitude/Indifference	Gratitude; a generous spirit

As St. John of Kronstadt tells us:

> The passions spur us on like cruel drivers, daily forcing us, through our love for earthly things, to act in opposition to the Lord and against our own true welfare, and to do that which is pleasing to the deluder, Satan. [212]

The contrasting list of virtues provides an overview of how to overcome these passions in order to pursue our vocation to holiness. As St. John of Kronstadt tells us: "The Lord does not dwell in a heart where greed and attachment to earthly benefits, pleasures, and

---

212 St. John of Kronstadt, *My Life in Christ*, Part 2, 124.

money hold supreme. This is daily proved by experience."[213] He adds, "O Lord, without you we can do nothing! Give us victory over our enemies and our passions. So be it!"[214]

Watching Out for the Small Things (the Thorns)

The challenge for us in cultivating a life of virtue is that we do not always realize when we are succumbing to temptation or even sinning. The Spiritual Fathers counsel us on watchfulness or sober vigilance (*nepsis*), to recognize the "thorns" that can choke the word so it bears no fruit.[215] Consider a few of Jesus's specific instructions to his disciples:

- "You have heard that it was said to your ancestors, 'You shall not kill; and whoever kills will be liable to judgment.' But I say to you, whoever is angry with his brother will be liable to judgment ..."[216]

  - Do I grow angry or impatient with others?

  - Do I find myself criticizing or frustrated with others?

- "You have heard that it was said, 'You shall not commit adultery.' But I say to you, everyone who looks at a woman with lust has already committed adultery with her in his heart."[217]

  - Do I have a complacent or commoditized view of sexuality?

  - Do I understand the dangers of pornography? Or

---

213 St. John of Kronstadt, *My Life in Christ*, Part 1, 235.
214 Ibid., 238.
215 See Matt. 13:22. "The seed sown among thorns is the one who hears the word, but then worldly anxiety and the lure of riches choke the word and it bears no fruit."
216 Matt. 5:21-22.
217 Matt. 5:27-28.

do I dismiss it as something "everyone does"?

- "If you forgive others their transgressions, your heavenly Father will forgive you. But if you do not forgive others, neither will your Father forgive your transgressions."[218]

  – Do I hold grudges long after something has happened?

  – Have I really forgiven others from my heart?

- "Stop judging, that you may not be judged. For as you judge, so will you be judged, and the measure with which you measure will be measured out to you."[219]

  – Do I judge others without realizing it?

  – Do I frequently criticize others? Do I usually see the negative instead of the positive?

  – Do I speak or concur when someone else criticizes another, or add my commentary?

  – Do I gossip or speak about others, stripping away the dignity of another person, who is also made in the divine image?

  – Do I cast others in a negative light?

  – Do I find faults in others? Do I denigrate others without realizing it?

  – Do I judge who is worthy of being part of the parish community? Do I label certain individuals or groups as "those people"? Do I stereotype others?

  – Do I look down upon those whom I judge have menial jobs?

218 Matt. 6:14-15.
219 Matt. 7:1-2.

- "Whoever wishes to be great among you shall be your servant; whoever wishes to be first among you shall be your slave."[220]

  - Do I find myself wanting to be in charge?

  - How often do I find myself wrestling with self-interest (looking out for me at the expense of others)?

  - Am I truly willing to serve others? All others? Do I judge who is worthy of my assistance?

- "Then they will answer and say, 'Lord, when did we see you hungry or thirsty or a stranger or naked or ill or in prison, and not minister to your needs?' He will answer them, 'Amen, I say to you, what you did not do for one of these least ones, you did not do for me.'"[221]

  - Do I treat all as neighbors as Jesus defined them? Consider the Parable of the Good Samaritan[222] which created a much broader definition of neighbor.

  - Am I moved to compassion when I see the homeless person under the bridge, the prostitute on the street corner, the addict collapsed on the sidewalk, or the destitute? Or, do I deliberately move to the other side of the road?

  - Do I feel an obligation to those who cannot find justice for themselves: the immigrant, the unborn, the homeless, or the undocumented worker?

  - How often do I find myself ignoring those who are in need?

---

220 Matt. 20:26-27.
221 Matt. 25:44-45.
222 See Luke 10:25-37.

- Do I sometimes judge people who are in need by saying it is their fault? Or, do I rationalize it away by saying, "That is not my problem"?

- Do I walk past Jesus silently crying out for help and not even recognize him?

We often have ingrained habits and do not realize when we lapse in small matters. Thus, we need to focus constantly on even our smallest failings, not allowing the thorns to choke out our seed of faith. Small habits left unchecked grow into bigger ones, which are even harder to root out. What did Jesus teach us in the Gospel? What example did he give us? This is the type of formation we are discussing, allowing Jesus to form our lives in alignment with his. A daily examination of conscience helps us consider the small ways we failed to follow the example of Christ. Or as Dorotheos of Gaza (505-565) wrote, "We really need to scrutinize our conduct every six hours and see in what way we have sinned since we sin so much and are so forgetful."[223] The more we become conscious of our small failings, the more authentically we can strive to overcome these challenges and cultivate a life of virtue. St. John of Kronstadt lamented, "What a great labor lies before every Christian to cleanse himself from the impurity and corruption of the passions!"[224]

Preparing for Struggles on the Journey to Eternal Blessedness

This discussion may seem like "boot camp" to some. However, this rigorous formation prepares us for the journey toward eternal blessedness, which, as the Spiritual Fathers and Mothers tell us, is one of constant struggle. They describe this as spiritual or unseen warfare and, as we survey the landscape around us, we recognize the enormity of the challenges. First, internally, we can find ourselves

---

223 Dorotheos of Gaza, *Discourses and Sayings*, 175. Discourse XI, "On Cutting Off Passionate Desires."
224 St. John of Kronstadt, *My Life in Christ*, Part 1, 262.

in the vise grip of certain passions or material desires. Or, we can find ourselves losing hope. The demons will find within us anything they can to fasten onto in order to pull us away from Christ.[225] These require continuous vigilance and attention to overcome. The Church Fathers also warn us that sometimes a passion with which we have struggled will disappear, deluding us into thinking we have conquered it. However, it can reappear, striking us when we are complacent. St. Paul described his own struggles in his Letter to the Romans.[226]

Externally, we know that the divide between the truth of the Gospel and the values of the dominant culture is increasing. Further, the culture can often encourage, promote, or enflame one or more of the passions (e.g., pride, greed, lust, etc.). As Elder Sophrony of Essex (1896-1993) wrote:

> Born into the world, we are bound to it by the strong bonds of kinship. We love the world. Within its bounds we fashion eternity. But we suffer in it—it cramps the love commanded of us.[227]

We cannot avoid living in the world; however, it does not mean we have to walk in its fallen ways or become enslaved by it. A deliberate effort is required to take the road less traveled, often demanding that we distance ourselves from people, places, or situations that could distract us from our vocation to holiness.

Jesus tells us that a condition of discipleship is to take up our cross daily,[228] which reminds us that his way[229] is the Way of the

---

225 See Ibid., 26.
226 See Rom. 7:18-25.
227 Sakharov, *We Shall See Him As He Is*, 101. Consider too 1 Pet. 5:8-9: "Be sober and vigilant. Your opponent the devil is prowling like a roaring lion looking for someone to devour. Resist him, steadfast in faith, knowing that your fellow believers throughout the world undergo the same sufferings."
228 See Luke 9:23.
229 See John 14:6. "Jesus said to him, 'I am the way and the truth and the life. No one comes to the Father except through me.'"

Cross. However, his way leads us to the truth of the Gospel and to life. There is no middle way. We have the choice of life in Christ (becoming adopted sons and daughters)[230] or withdrawal from God and his graces, which ultimately leads us to listlessness, darkness, and despair.[231] God gives us the freedom to choose and will respect the decision we make. To attain eternal blessedness, we must also realize that every person "created in the divine image will have to cross the threshold of suffering—voluntary suffering for the sake of holy love. Without this testing of our freedom, we cannot realize ourselves as truly free persons."[232] At the same time, we must learn to love as God loves in order to prepare ourselves for union with him. This is the mystery Christ revealed to us.[233]

If we were to summarize the lessons of being formed in Christ, they would be threefold: humility; obedience, or surrender of self-will to the Divine will; and patient endurance.[234] In terms of the latter, Jesus never condemned anyone. He encouraged, healed, embraced the lowly, cautioned against consequences of not following him, wept over the unrepentant, forgave, and was silent amid scourging and insults. As he taught his disciples, "But I say to you, offer no resistance to one who is evil."[235] This is the model for us to follow and, through formation, we learn to increasingly live as Jesus showed us.

The vocation to holiness and the associated incremental striving for change (*theosis*) require significant effort and patience. It is not mastered in a single instance; rather, it is honed over our lifetime on earth and can only reach perfection in the life to come at the Resurrection of the Dead. We need to take it one step at a time and

---

230 See Gal. 4:5.

231 See Matt. 22:13-14.

232 See Sakharov, *We Shall See Him As He Is*, 93-94. St. John of Kronstadt would add that our current state of affairs "foreshadows the future. The difference is only one of degree—for the righteous, the future will be the fullness of eternal glory, for sinners the fullness of everlasting torment." See *My Life in Christ*, Part 1, 49.

233 Ibid., 94.

234 See Matt. 24:12-13. "Because of the increase of evildoing, the love of many will grow cold. But the one who perseveres to the end will be saved."

235 Matt. 5:38.

realize that, as humans, there will be times when we fail. As one Athonite spiritual elder described it, sometimes we are sailing when the wind blows and other times the labor of rowing is needed.[236] Translation: We can anticipate times of greater struggle, either in prayer or simply with regard to the challenges of life. We are given what we need as "our daily bread" in order to become less dependent on self and more reliant on God. This is all predicated on human-divine collaboration (*synergeia*), and involves spiritual practices such as asceticism and detachment, cultivating a life of virtue, a regular discipline of prayer, and loving our neighbor as a concrete expression of our love for God. Salvation cannot be achieved apart from God.

Also, *synergeia* is best illustrated by what happened after the disciples completed their formation (at the Ascension) and when they received the Holy Spirit at Pentecost. Their preparation, in essence, was to receive the Holy Spirit, after which their lives were never the same. This is what we can expect when we accept the invitation to "follow me" and do what Jesus asks: "Be with me. Let me lead you, guide you, teach you. Let me give you strength. Surrender yourself to me and I will take care of everything."

With Jesus, we have life and eternal blessedness. Without Jesus, we lose life.

> "Everyone who listens to these words of mine and acts on them will be like a wise man who built his house on rock. The rain fell, the floods came, and the winds blew and buffeted the house. But it did not collapse; it had been set solidly on rock.
>
> "And everyone who listens to these words of mine but does not act on them will be like a fool who built his house on sand. The rain fell, the floods came, and the

---

236 See Metropolitan Hierotheos of Nafpaktos, *A Night in the Desert of the Holy Mountain*, 86.

winds blew and buffeted the house. And it collapsed and was completely ruined."[237]

Our formation is intended to build a spiritual house on rock, one that will not collapse during times of trial, temptation, or tribulations. Once we have proven our steadfastness, God will make his dwelling with us.[238]

Reflection for Conference No. 3: St. Nephon's Advice to a Young Man

"My child, if you want to live amongst the people, you must watch the following: Do not criticize anyone at all; do not ridicule anyone; do not become angry; do not despise anyone. Be very careful not to say 'so-and-so lives virtuously,' or 'so-and-so lives immorally,' because this is exactly what 'judge not' (Matt. 7:1) means. Look at everyone in the same way, with the same disposition, the same thought, with a simple heart. Accept them as you would accept Christ. Don't open your ears to a person who judges. More so, don't be happy nor agree with whatever he says, but keep your mouth shut. In other words, be slow to speak but quick to pray. Neither condemn in your thoughts the one who judges. Of course he is doing something wrong. But you should look at your own shortcomings and criticize only yourself."

"Father," observed the youth, "what you told me is for the seasoned fighters. How will I, worthless that I am, be able to attain that in order to please God?"

"My son, if youth has humility and purity, it is enough.

---

237 Matt. 7:24-27.
238 See Sakharov, *We Shall See Him As He Is*, 85. See also John 14:23. "Whoever loves me will keep my word, and my Father will love him, and we will come to him and make our dwelling with him."

God asks nothing else of it. For this reason, my lad, be pure and humble. Place yourself beneath everyone else. Then truly you will live in fellowship with Christ."

An Ascetic Bishop: Stories, Sermons, and Prayers of St. Nephon. 2nd ed. Translated by Jeannie Gentithes and Archimandrite Ignatios Apostololopoulos, 161-163. Florence, AZ: St. Anthony's Monastery, 2015.

Conference No. 3 (alternative reflection): "To Be Christian"

For to be Christian is to be crucified, in this time and in any time since Christ came for the first time. His life is the example—and warning—to us all. We must be crucified personally, mystically; for crucifixion is the only path to resurrection.

If we would rise with Christ, we must first be humbled with him—even to the ultimate humiliation, being devoured and spit forth by the uncomprehending world …

No wonder then, that it is hard to be a Christian— it is not hard, it is impossible … And that is why we constantly rebel, try to make life easier, try to be half-Christian, try to make the best of both worlds.

We must ultimately choose—our [happiness] lies in one world or the other, not both. God gives us the strength to pursue the path to crucifixion; there is no other way to be Christian.

Fr. Seraphim Rose (1934-82), from his journal. Hieromonk Damascene. *Father Seraphim Rose: His Life and His Works.* 3rd rev. ed. Platina, CA: St. Herman of Alaska Brotherhood, 2010.

Reflection Questions

1. What can I do to simplify my life? What attachments do I have? What is necessary; what can I do without?

2. Do I struggle with the small sins that can choke my faith? Am I aware of my habits?

3. Do I avoid the way of the world? Or do I find myself swept along with what others around me are doing?

4. Do I struggle with humility? What are my specific struggles?

5. What lessons can I learn from the examples of Christ? How can I put them into practice?

6. As Matthew Kelly asks, "What are the daily routines and rituals that keep you grounded and focused on what matters most each day? Do you notice the difference between the days when you are faithful to those habits and other days when you neglect them?"[239]

Making a Commitment to Formation

Like any exercise program, the formation we described above requires a commitment, practice, and discipline. As part of his Call to Spiritual Renewal in 2019, His Grace Bishop Milan Lach, SJ of the Eparchy of Parma, asked the faithful to commit to one or more spiritual practices during the year. We would encourage our retreat participants to do likewise.

---

239 Matthew Kelly, *Rediscover the Saints*, 96. Note that this is essentially The Art of Spiritual Life.

Suggested Formation Practices
(from the Eparchy of Parma Pledge Card)

- ☐ Attend liturgy every Sunday and Holy Day.
- ☐ Fast every Friday.
- ☐ Visit the Mystery of Repentance at least during the four fasting periods of the year.
- ☐ Pray every morning and evening.
- ☐ Practice a work of charity every day.
- ☐ Read one chapter from the New Testament every day.

Additional Formation Practices to Consider

- ☐ Specific actions I can take to simplify my life (specify).
- ☐ Daily practice of the Jesus Prayer for a set interval of time.
- ☐ Fast every Wednesday and Friday.
- ☐ More frequent reception of Eucharist over and above Sundays and Holy Days. Be strengthened by the Real Presence of Christ.
- ☐ Spiritual reading of the Fathers of the Church. Perhaps pick a specific Father or Mother and spend time reading and learning about his or her life as model for my own life.
- ☐ Daily examination of conscience and more frequent visits to the Mystery of Repentance (monthly, weekly, etc.) in order to keep the small sins from choking my spiritual life.

"The means to confirm and strengthen Christian hope are prayer, especially frequent and sincere prayer, confession of our sins, frequent reading of the Word of God, and, above all, frequent communion of the holy and life-giving sacraments of the Body and Blood of Christ."[240]

---

240 St. John of Kronstadt, *The Spiritual Counsels of Fr. John of Kronstadt*, ed. W. Jardine Grisbrooke (Crestwood, NY: St. Vladimir's Seminary Press, 1981), 5.

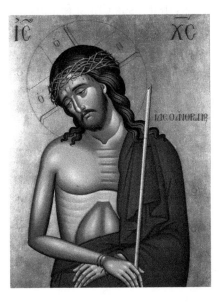

Icon of Christ the Bridegroom. Sometimes called Extreme Humility.
Christ is the divine Bridegroom of the Church (see Isaiah 54:5). The
Bridegroom is also the central image of the Parable of the Ten Virgins
(Matt. 25:1-13). Christ the Bridegroom suffered for his bride, the Church.

Jesus describes himself as "the way" to the Father (John 14:6), and he tells us, "If anyone wishes to come after me, he must deny himself and take up his cross daily and follow me" (Luke 9:23). Our formation by Christ, our following his example, is one of disciplining ourselves to surrender completely to the Divine will, to unconditionally follow the will of the Father. This is the only way to eternal blessedness. The icon of Christ the Bridegroom (extreme humility) reminds us of what it means to come after Christ, that his way is the Way of the Cross. However, Jesus will also remain with us and strengthen us on the journey.

As a Benedictine monk wrote, "I am not at all astonished at the opposition and difficulties that you are meeting at this moment. I was expecting them. God's best graces must be purchased by suffering, and it is upon the cross that Jesus Christ founds his great works."[241]

---

241 Blessed Columba Marmion, "Giving without Cost," *Magnificat*, 21/5 (July 2019), 157-158. Blessed Columba (1858-1923) was abbot of the Benedictine abbey of Maredsous, Belgium.

Transformation

"I have been crucified with Christ, yet I live, no longer I, but Christ
lives in me; insofar as I now live in the flesh, I live by faith in the
Son of God who has loved me and given himself up for me."
(Gal. 2:19-20)

"It is time that Christians should understand the Lord, should
understand what he requires of us—namely, a pure heart."[242]
(St. John of Kronstadt)

"A saint is distinguished by his humility and love."[243]
(Monk Moses of Mount Athos)

Introduction to the Conference

Throughout this retreat, we have examined the concept of a vocation to holiness to which every person is called. This involves remaining with Christ, experiencing him through our encounters, and being taught and formed by him in order to gain eternal blessedness, which is sharing in the life of the Holy Trinity. Only Christ is the true source of life, the way leading to eternal blessedness. He is the vine and we are the branches; we have life through him.[244] Without Christ, we have no life within us. Self-reliance is a barren faith.

The first step in our vocation to holiness is to say "yes" to Jesus's command, "Follow me." However, this is just the beginning. We must also commit to the ongoing journey and to develop a deeper relationship with Jesus Christ. We need to learn humility, obedience

---

242 St. John of Kronstadt, *My Life in Christ*, Part 1, 198.
243 Monk Moses, *Holiness: Is It Attainable Today?*, 4.
244 John 15:1-6.

(surrender to the Divine will), and patient endurance. We need to be firmly rooted to him through prayer. However, in the final analysis, it is not about our encounters with Christ or the formation itself. Rather, it is about who we become because of them. Do we become more Christ-like? As Elder Sophrony of Essex said, "*Theosis* means that in every situation in our life we react as Christ reacted."

The first apostles heard the voice of Jesus. They made the radical decision to follow him. They went through a period of formation, learning and listening to Jesus's words and observing his examples. To be sure, there were many failings, weaknesses in faith, and even betrayals along the way. However, at Pentecost when they received the Holy Spirit, this period of formation and Life in Christ bore abundant fruit. Through this divine-human collaboration (*synergeia*), the Church was born. Thus, the desire to follow Christ and persistence are prerequisites.

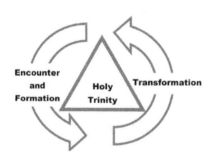

Encounters with and formation by Christ lead us to transformation,[245] which in turn prepares us for eternal blessedness, drawing us into the life of the Holy Trinity. This transformation is incremental (*theosis*), beginning in this life and completed in the life to come at the Resurrection of the Dead.

Opening Gospel Passage

Read: Matt. 5:3-12 (The Beatitudes) or

Luke 10:25-37 (Parable of the Good Samaritan).

---

245 See Rom. 5:5. "The love of God has been poured out into our hearts by the Holy Spirit that has been given to us." This is the foundation for divine-human collaboration (*synergeia*), which is critical to salvation and eternal blessedness. Achievement of salvation is beyond human capability and depends solely on the goodness of God who offers it freely as a gift ("the offer of salvation").

Living Our Vocation to Holiness

Do our lives bear witness to our faith? Do we live as authentic disciples of Jesus? These are questions we ask ourselves to gauge progress on the spiritual journey. Jesus instructs his disciples:

> "I give you a new commandment: love one another. As I have loved you, so you also should love one another. This is how all will know that you are my disciples, if you have love for one another."[246]

Jesus speaks of the primacy of love, saying this will be how all will recognize who his disciples are. He reiterates this message when discussing the Greatest Commandment[247]: "The second is like it: You shall love your neighbor as yourself."[248] This love of God is manifested in love of neighbor. We love the God we cannot see by loving our neighbor, whom we can see, and who is made in the divine image just as we are.[249] As Mother Teresa of Calcutta wrote, "Radiate the joy of belonging to God, of living with him and being his."[250] So, love is an essential attribute of God and one that should become part of who we are as followers of Jesus. A deep-seated relationship with Christ should create a fire within us, a fire that can be experienced by others.

St. Isaac the Syrian tells us:

> Love the poor, that through them you many also find mercy. Bear noisome smells of the sick without disgust, and especially of the poor, since you too are wrapped about with a body. Do not rebuke those who

---

246 John 13:34-35.
247 See Matt. 22:34-40.
248 Matt. 22:39.
249 See 1 John 4:20. "If anyone says, "I love God," but hates his brother, he is a liar; for whoever does not love a brother whom he has seen cannot love God whom he has not seen."
250 Mother Teresa of Calcutta, *Love: A Fruit Always in Season*, ed. Dorothy S. Hunt (San Francisco, CA: Ignatius Press, 1987), 58.

are afflicted in heart, lest you be scourged with the selfsame rod as theirs: then you will seek consolation and find none. Do not disdain those who are deformed from birth, because all of us will go to the grave equally privileged. Love sinners, but hate their works; and do not despise them their faults, lest you be tempted by the same. Remember that you share the earthly nature of Adam and that you are clothed with his infirmity. Do not reprove those who are in need of your prayer, and do not withhold tender words of comfort from them, lest they perish and their souls be required of you...[251]

St. Isaac also tells us, "There are three ways every rational soul can draw [near] to God: by fervency of faith,[252] by fear,[253] and by the Lord's chastisements. No man can draw [near] to the love of God if one of these three does not lead the way."[254] We can observe these characteristics in many of the Spiritual Fathers and Mothers who have gone before us. How about us? Is our faith grounded on rock?[255]

Do we live as people of faith? Do we make God first in our lives? Do we make Christ's priorities our own? In times of affliction or troubles, do we live as people of hope? Or, do we collapse and become swept away like the house built on sand? Do we live with a divinely inspired purpose? Do our lives reflect the beauty of our Creator, in whose image we were created and whose image is impressed within each of us? Have we established an "inner dwelling" for the Holy Spirit? This dwelling is established through attitude (desire, the "yes" to the call) and maintaining the disciplines of the spiritual life, living in conformity with Christ (*praxis*). Consider this in terms of patience

---

251 *The Ascetical Homilies of Saint Isaac the Syrian*, 167. Homily Five.
252 See *The Ascetical Homilies of Isaac the Syrian*, 161. Homily Five. St. Isaac would describe this as knocking "persistently at his door."
253 As discussed previously, fear in this sense means a reverential awe for God.
254 *The Ascetical Homilies of Saint Isaac the Syrian*, 169. Homily Six.
255 See Matt. 7:24-29.

and persistence (endurance). Patience is the willingness to "stay the course," to continue to listen to the voice of God. Persistence is the tangible faithfulness to continue the *praxis*, the incremental effort or work that makes "staying the course" possible.[256]

If we truly live as Christians, we likely will stand in stark contrast to the values of the dominant culture. And, we need to be okay with this. Otherwise, our relationship with Christ can be easily derailed, swept away by the popular tide. We cannot be complacent, straddling the fence between following Christ and the truth of the Gospel on one hand, and the messages, attitudes, and practices popularized by secular society on the other. There is no such thing as a "Comfort Catholic." We need to choose which master we will serve.[257]

As Archbishop Charles J. Chaput of Philadelphia (1944—) wrote:

> Living in Christ requires daily conversion, discipleship, and transformation. Becoming a Christian and living in Christ imply a lifetime of growing in Christ. The water of Baptism gives life to the seed in our hearts that is Jesus Christ. The more the seed grows—the more we nourish and cultivate it through the sacraments, prayer, and apostolic action—the more we grow *into* Christ. We were made to do that. We were made to grow and bear the fruit of cooperating with Jesus in redeeming and sanctifying the world.[258]

As Jesus tells us:

> "You are the light of the world. A city set on a mountain cannot be hidden. Nor do they light a lamp and then put it under a bushel basket; it is set on a lampstand,

---

256 See Keller, *Desert Banquet*, 147.
257 See Matt. 6:24. "No one can serve two masters. He will either hate one or love the other, or be devoted to one and despise the other. You cannot serve God and mammon."
258 Chaput, *Living the Catholic Faith*, 44.

> where it gives light to all in the house. Just so, your
> light must shine before others, that they may see your
> good deeds and glorify your heavenly Father."[259]

Our vocation to holiness makes us disciples of Christ, and we are called to share our faith with others through the witness of our lives. We must be the light in the midst of the darkness in a world that desires to extinguish it.

The reality we face is that, like the apostles at Pentecost, the world is increasingly hostile to Christianity. The sanctity and fundamental dignity of human life is being compromised, especially with increasingly liberal abortion laws; the sanctity of marriage is questioned; families, the fundamental cell of society, are in crisis; and there is an increasing divide between rich and poor, with increasing apathy toward those in need. Constructive dialogue among our elected officials has denigrated to personal agendas. Race relations and community outreach have experienced serious setbacks. Religious civil liberties and freedoms, guaranteed in the Constitution of the United States, are being questioned, such as through the mandated health care debate, and there is an effort to place increasing restrictions on the Church, including questioning the sacred seal of Confession. As Msgr. Charles Pope warned in 2016, "Comfort Catholicism has to go."[260] We need to prepare ourselves for persecution, because the future situation is likely to become increasingly hostile as the secular values of society drift farther away from Gospel truths.

Internally, we also face challenges as some within the Church create ambiguity and confusion by trying to give into the spirit of the age, trying to widen the narrow gate.[261] "While Christians are dying for their faith and their fidelity to Jesus, in the West, men of

---

259 Matt. 5:14-16.
260 See Msgr. Charles Pope, "Comfort Catholicism Has to Go; It is Time to Prepare for Persecution," *National Catholic Register* online (August 21, 2016).
261 See Luke 13:24. Jesus says, "Strive to enter through the narrow door."

the Church are trying to reduce the requirements of the Gospel to a minimum,"[262] wrote Cardinal Sarah. Efforts to widen the gate are seen by attempts to water down orthodox teaching or trying to minimize or trivialize the requirements of salvation—an attempt to accommodate or compromise with the spirit of the age. It is important to provide clarity in this regard. Jesus desires the salvation of *all*. We see this in the Apostolic Church, wherein the apostles were concerned with the Greek-speaking widows.[263] St. Paul spent his entire missionary efforts of evangelization on the Greek-speaking world. The fishermen cast a wide net to catch the whole world.[264] Thus, the *offer* of salvation itself is not narrow.

The challenge is in *accepting* the offer of salvation.[265] "All are welcome in the Church, but on Christ's terms, not our own," said Francis Cardinal George, OMI of Chicago (1937-2015). The truth of the Gospel does not change with the spirit of the age. "Jesus Christ is the same yesterday, today, and forever."[266] As Pope Paul VI wrote:

> There is no true evangelization if the name, the teaching, the life, the promises, the kingdom, and the mystery of Jesus of Nazareth, the Son of God, are not proclaimed.[267]

Jesus himself said the *way* to salvation is narrow, whereas the

---

262 Robert Cardinal Sarah, in conversation with Nicolas Diat, *God or Nothing: A Conversation on Faith*, transl. Michael J. Miller (San Francisco, CA: Ignatius Press, 2015), 280.

263 See Acts 6:1-6. The call of the first deacons was to serve those who were marginalized.

264 See the Troparion of Pentecost Sunday, *The Divine Liturgies of Our Holy Father John Chrysostom*, 204-205. "You have shown the fishermen to be all wise.... Through them you have caught the whole world in your net."

265 See Pope Francis, *Evangelii Gaudium* (Rome: Libreria Editrice Vaticana, 2013), no. 1. "The Joy of the Gospel fills the hearts and lives of *all* who encounter Jesus. *Those who accept his offer of salvation* are set free from sin, sorrow, inner emptiness and loneliness. With Christ joy is constantly born anew." (Emphasis added.)

266 Heb. 13:8.

267 Pope Paul VI, *Evangelii Nuntiandi* (Rome: Libreria Editrice Vaticana, 1975), no. 22.

wide gate leads to destruction.[268] Herein lies the challenge for many when comparing the Gospel truth with the dominant culture, trying to find compromises or revise the teachings (trying to widen the narrow gate). However, consider the time of Jesus. His teachings were considered radical and the decision to follow him required radical change (conversion of heart). People struggled then, too. Recall how the crowds murmured: "This teaching is hard; who can accept it?"[269] Are we any more able to accept the teachings of Jesus today? Alone, it is impossible. With God, all things are possible.[270] Bottom line: Humanity needs God.

Accordingly, by allowing Jesus to form, guide, and strengthen us, we strive to build our spiritual house on a solid foundation. We want to remain with Christ, deeply rooted in our relationship with him, the true source of life, in order to resist the temptations and compromises advocated by the spirit of the age, especially as the gap between the truth of the Gospel and messages of secular society grows ever wider. Our vocation to holiness has many challenges and struggles; transformation is incremental and requires patience and persistence. However, the world desperately needs the light of authentic Christian witness that stands in stark contrast to the direction of the current age.

Beware of Illusions[271]

In our vocation to holiness, we must beware of illusions that cause us to believe we are already living a good life or that there is an easier way to achieve eternal blessedness. Throughout this retreat, we said

---

268 See Matt. 7:13-14. "Enter through the narrow gate; for the gate is wide and the road broad that leads to destruction, and those who enter through it are many. How narrow the gate and restricted the road that leads to life. And those who find are few."

269 John 6:60.

270 See Matt. 19:26. "For human beings this is impossible, but for God all things are possible." This reminds us of the importance of divine-human collaboration (*synergeia*) in order for us to achieve salvation.

271 This section was greatly influenced by a homily of Fr. Miron Kerul-Kmec, St. Nicholas Byzantine Catholic Church, Barberton, Ohio (September 1, 2019). https://artofspirituallife. podbean.com/e/september-1-2019-1567374085/.

that there is no middle way between the truth of the Gospel and the spirit of the age. However, a phenomenon we may have observed is complacency, where a person says, "I am good enough. I live a good life and help others. I have done enough to get to heaven; I don't need to do anything more." This illusion creates pleasant thoughts, and we may come to think salvation is easy; we are already well on the way. However, in many respects this is a rejection of the ongoing journey of transformation (*theosis*), tantamount to saying, "I have already arrived," when in fact the journey is far from over.[272] This mindset also implies we can take salvation into our own hands or that we can dilute the teachings of Jesus ("close enough"). In reality, this is a delusion rooted within the passion of pride. As discussed in Conference No. 3, the demons will find within us anything they can fasten onto in order to pull us away from Christ. Accordingly, complacency is one snare that can entrap us, preventing us from being completely dependent on God. Further, the Church Fathers throughout the ages have told us that we must discern each day what is going in our hearts and to recognize these traps.

We might ask why such thinking seems to persist in our current culture. The seeds go back to the European Enlightenment, an intellectual and philosophical movement that dominated the ideas of Europe in the eighteenth century, and is still reflected in our societal consciousness today. The Enlightenment fostered a belief in the inherent goodness of humanity and confidence that human beings had the capacity for greatness within themselves, dismissing the role of God (reason over faith). Couple this with the fact that a number of Protestant denominations in recent times have attempted to compromise their teachings to accommodate the spirit of the age, even taking positions in moral theology that certain matters are ones of personal conscience (e.g., abortion is only wrong if my conscience tells me it is wrong). Pope Francis warns in his apostolic exhortation,

---

272 Consider the Parable of the Rich Fool (Luke 12:16-21). The fool says, "Now as for you, you have so many good things stored up for many years, rest, eat, drink, be merry!" This is a good illustration of the dangers of complacency.

Choosing Life in Christ

Gaudete et Exsultate (On the Call to Holiness in Today's World), about modern Pelagianism.[273] This was a heresy in the Early Church, named after the British monk Pelagius (354-420), that taught humanity could choose the good and achieve salvation through individual efforts and, most notably, *without* divine assistance. The illusion of complacency ("good enough") is reflective of this Pelagianism. Yet, Jesus himself is clear, "Without me you can do nothing."[274] Accordingly, we have cultural conditions that can predispose us to such illusions that salvation is within our individual means and/or that the road is really not that difficult. The latter is a corollary to efforts to widen the narrow gate (see above).

In a time when we see efforts to water down Christian teaching to accommodate the spirt of the age, we need to be cautious, discerning these snares and remaining firmly rooted in the teachings of Jesus. The author of the Letter to Hebrews warns, "Do not be carried away by all kinds of strange teaching."[275]

As an example, let us consider the rich young man we discussed in Conference No. 1, who asks Jesus, "Teacher, what good must I do to gain eternal life?"[276] To be certain, the rich young man is asking the right question, indeed the most important question, desiring the eternal blessedness promised by God. And Jesus gives him an answer with regard to the requirements, keeping the commandments[277] and, when he questioned what was still lacking, was told that to be *perfect*, he must sell all that he had, give the money to the poor, and follow him.[278] Throughout his teachings, Jesus never compromised on the terms and conditions of discipleship. He set the standards[279] and

---

273 See Pope Francis, *Gaudete et Exsultate* (Rome: Libreria Editrice Vaticana, 2019), no. 47-62.
274 John 15:5.
275 Heb. 13:9.
276 Matt. 19:16.
277 Matt. 19:17-19.
278 Matt. 19:21.
279 See Matt. 5:48. "So be perfect, just as your Heavenly Father is perfect." This is the standard set by Jesus, which is impossible to achieve without divine assistance. That is why the delusion of "good enough" erodes the fundamental teachings of Jesus.

these can only be achieved with divine assistance.[280]

In Conference No. 3, we discussed the fact that God gives us the freedom to choose and will respect our decision. Consider what happened when the rich young man heard Jesus's answer as to what was still lacking. "He went away sad, for he had many possessions."[281] What did Jesus do? He did not chase after the young man, saying, "Wait! May be we can relax the standards a bit." He did not water down the requirements of discipleship and he respected the free-will decision of the young man, who could not accept these requirements. As Elder Porphyrios wrote, "[God] also respects our freedom. He does not pressure us."[282]

When evaluating our choice to follow Christ, we must understand that there is no compromise or relaxing of standards to accommodate the spirit of the age. Jesus said, "How narrow the gate and constricted the road that leads to life. And those who find it are few."[283] We must constantly strive to follow the example and teachings he gave to us, seeking to align our lives with his, and allowing him to guide us. There are many traps; complacency or referring to what is acceptable in the dominant culture take us away from the Source of Life. We cannot be deluded into thinking salvation is easy, because Jesus tells us his way is the Way of the Cross.[284] There is no room for "good enough," or a lukewarm faith. In fact, in the Book of Revelation there is a warning: "Because you are lukewarm, neither hot nor cold, I will spit you out of my mouth."[285] There is no middle way, only snares to entrap us into an illusion there is an easier way to achieve the goal we

---

280 See Matt 19:16. "For human beings this is impossible, but for God all things are possible." Thus, it is impossible to achieve salvation without divine assistance (*synergeia*).

281 Matt. 19:22.

282 Elder Porphyrios, *Wounded by Love*, 192.

283 Matt. 7:14.

284 The cross represents the ultimate act of love modeled by Jesus. St. John of Kronstadt reminds us, "It is impossible to imagine and think of the cross without thinking of love. Where the cross is, there is love. In the Church, you see crosses everywhere and on everything, in order that everything should remind you that you are in the church of the God of love, in the church of Love Himself, crucified for us." See *My Life in Christ*—Part 1, 198.

285 Rev. 3:16.

desire. St. John of Kronstadt warns us about such illusions:

> O Man! Recognize your spiritual misfortune, and steadfastly, continually pray to the Savior of men to save you from it. Do not say to yourself, "I am not in danger; I am not in misery; I do not need to pray much and often to be saved from a misfortune which I do not even understand or know." This is the very misfortune, that you, being in the greatest misery, do not know your misfortune. This misfortune is your sinfulness.[286]

Our vocation to holiness involves a continuous renouncing of reliance on self and making ourselves reliant on God and his infinite mercy. This radical dependence stands in stark contrast to the spirit of the age and it is by no means easy. However, we cannot cease to struggle, to pray, to fast, and wage spiritual warfare until our last breath, because our incremental transformation will not end until the Resurrection of the Dead.

> When Christ is in our heart, we are content with everything. Even discomfort becomes the greatest comfort, bitterness becomes sweet, poverty becomes wealth, hunger becomes plenty, and sorrow becomes joy! But when Christ is not in our heart, then we are not content with anything, we find happiness in nothing—not in health, not in comfort, not in ranks and honors, not in amusements, not in rich palaces, not in a luxurious table, covered with all manner food and drink, not in rich clothing—in nothing! *O, how necessary for man is Christ, the Life-giver and Savior of our souls!* How necessary it is for us to hunger and thirst, to sleep less, to dress more simply, and to bear everything with a quiet, peaceful, patient, meek

---

286 St. John of Kronstadt, *My Life in Christ*, Part 2, 156.

spirit for Christ's sake, so that he will dwell in us. The wicked fowler of our souls—the devil—seeks at every moment to ensnare our souls, trying to wound us by some sin or passion, searching for ways he can implant some sinful habit or passion more firmly within us, striving to make the salvation of our soul as difficult as possible, desiring to produce in us a coldness toward God, toward holy things, toward the Church, toward eternity, and toward mankind.[287]

Let us recognize that complacency is a snare of the demons, a weed being sown, to snatch our hearts away from Christ and to derail our vocation to holiness. We must remain ever vigilant against delusions (*nepsis*), strive to draw closer to Christ, and frequently discern whether we are on the right path. Through our continuous encounters and ongoing formation by Jesus, we will be gradually transformed into the likeness of Christ (*theosis*), drawing ever closer to eternal blessedness and sharing in the life of the Holy Trinity.

Living Our Vocation to Holiness in Community (Missionary Discipleship)

Individual transformation should also lead to the transformation of our faith communities. We need to create the right environment for ourselves and for others to nurture a vocation to holiness. The pastor of Holy Trinity Ukrainian Greek Catholic Church in Carnegie, Pennsylvania, has this message on his parish's website:

God made us to be eternally happy with him, beginning in this age and continuing forever in the endless age to come. Our parish exists to help you achieve that single goal: eternal happiness with God.

---

287 St. John of Kronstadt, *My Life in Christ*, Part 1, 147. Italics added by the author.

> In the history of the world, we believe there is only one way to do that and it is through knowing and loving Jesus Christ.[288]

The single goal of our parishes is to assist parishioners on the journey to eternal blessedness. This is the genuine mission of the Church.[289] Eternal happiness or even lasting happiness cannot be gained through finite or temporary things. The pastor describes Jesus as the way to achieve eternal happiness, and we do this by coming to know and love Jesus Christ.

The question for us is whether our parish lives up to that purpose. Does it exist to help people achieve the single goal of our life? Are we creating an environment that is supportive of growth in the spiritual life? Are we nurturing one another to strive for holiness? Is Christ authentically present in our church today, not just in the tabernacle, but truly alive in the hearts of those present? Are people's hearts on fire for love of Jesus? If not, what am I willing to do about it? We have a collective responsibility for one another as members of the body of Christ.[290]

The reality is that we do not undertake the spiritual journey alone. We are intended to do this as a community of believers. In *Evangelii Gaudium*, Pope Francis elaborates on the concept of "spiritual accompaniment"—that we support one another, "removing our sandals before others in humility," walking with each other "in a steady and reassuring manner, reflecting our closeness and a compassionate gaze which heals, liberates, and encourages our growth in the Christian life."[291] So how can I support others in my own community to persevere on the journey? One of the reasons for

288 Fr. Jason Charron, "About Us," Holy Trinity Ukrainian Catholic Church, Carnegie, PA, http://www. http://htucc.com/about.htm.
289 See Robert Cardinal Sarah, *The Day is Now Far Spent*, 256. The "genuine mission of the Church … consists essentially of bringing men to God and enabling man's heart to become a sacred temple again, the temple and dwelling place of God."
290 See also Rom. 12:5. "So we, though many, are one Body in Christ and individually parts of one another."
291 See Pope Francis, *Evangelii Gaudium*, nos. 169-170.

growing disaffiliation[292] by young Catholics is lack of companions on the spiritual journey.[293] How can I reach out to those who greatly need to encounter Jesus but have no idea who he really is? How can we inspire our young people to embrace friendship with the Lord Jesus, who is the answer to the question that is every human life?[294] How do we evangelize those who have rejected the Church or organized religion in general? We are called to care for the well-being of all our brothers and sisters. Jesus desires to save all.

Perhaps we should consider what Pope Francis has encouraged us to become, "a community of missionary disciples,"[295] to be in a constant state of mission to joyfully make Christ known to others so all will have a deeper relationship with the Risen Jesus. We can find ways to grow individually, communally, and evangelically, and reach out to others who are not practicing the Christian faith. Something happened at Pentecost, and we are entrusted with the mission to continue spreading the Good News, to pass on the spiritual treasures entrusted to us. We are stewards of the mysteries and treasures of faith. Most importantly, we cannot overlook our youth who are the future of our Church and who are hungry to know their faith and its relevance in their lives.

We also cannot understate the sense of urgency for this work. There has been significant complacency with respect to the faith that has been handed down to us. Statistics tell us that for every million children in the United States who are baptized and receive First Holy Communion, only 750,000 are confirmed (in the Western

---

292 Disaffiliation means more than people who no longer come to church on Sunday. These are people who no longer identify themselves as Catholics. These are the "nones" to which Bishop Robert Barron refers.

293 Catholic News Service, "Young Adults Want to be Heard by the Church, Study Finds," *Texas Catholic Herald*, January 23, 2018, 2. Reference is made to the survey contained in Robert J. McCarty and John M. Vitek, *Going, Going, Gone: The Dynamics of Disaffiliation in Young Catholics* (Winona, MN: St. Mary's Press, 2017). This survey was conducted from 2015-2017.

294 George Weigel, "Eastern Catholics and the Universal Church, *First Things* online (June 6, 2019), www.firstthings.com/web-exclusive/2019/06/eastern-catholics-and-the-universal-church. Weigel describes this as "perhaps the greatest challenge you will face as a Church of the New Evangelization."

295 Pope Francis, *Evangelii Gaudium*, no. 24.

Church), and only 110,000 remain active in their faith by young adulthood. This is a crisis of faith of epidemic proportions. Much of the disillusionment and frustration experienced by our youth is that their questions of faith are not answered or they never had a chance to ask them in the first place.[296] Many may conclude that the Church is essentially about following prescribed rules without ever having a genuine experience of faith (an encounter with God) or understanding of the underlying teachings associated with the Gospel (in other words, proper formation versus simply catechesis). The former is a superficial faith (the seed that fell on the path, or rocky ground, or among thorns) versus a genuine interior faith (seed that fell on good soil).[297] Our challenge is to continue to cultivate and enrich the soil through genuine dialogue and engagement with our faith, specifically focused on encounter with the Risen Jesus, his teachings, and helping others to remain with him, be formed and guided by him, and strengthened by him. It is easy in our society today to become complacent with respect to our responsibilities of passing on the deposit of faith to the next generation.

In his pastoral letter dated January 6, 2019, His Grace Bishop Milan Lach, SJ of the Eparchy of Parma, references St. Theophan the Recluse, who describes what happens when the grace given at baptism is not preserved. The consequences are:

1. Leaving the Church and its grace-giving means, which starves the root of the Christian life, disconnecting it from its sources. In this way, it wilts, just as a flower does when it is not watered.

2. Forgetting the main goal of life: People do not have the direction and lack the means to achieve union with God.

3. Neglecting the spiritual life: Prayer, fear of God, and conscience are overshadowed by earthly cares.

---

296 Catholic News Service, "Young Adults Want to be Heard by the Church, Study Finds."
297 See the Parable of the Sower: Matt. 13:1-9; 18-23, Mark 4:1-9; 13-20, and Luke 8:4-8; 11-15.

4.   Neglecting to put into practice Christian principles and God's way of life.[298]

Losing the graces received at Baptism is separation from Christ, the true source of life. That is why people who do not possess faith often experience listlessness, despair, and despondency, not being able to find a sense of purpose or fulfillment. "In a culture drenched in hedonism and materialism, people are as hungry as ever for another path, a spiritual path."[299]

The crisis of faith also leads to a loss of hope. The cause of this crisis, though, is not because structured religion or the Church has lost meaning, as some argue. Rather, as Christians, we have forgotten how to be "mystics,"[300]—those attuned to the divine presence through genuine encounter. Many have lost or have not been exposed to one of the most fundamental components of the spiritual life: the ability to encounter Jesus through prayer. Simply put, we as a Church and a society do not know how to pray as we should.[301] In many cases, it seems as if personal prayer has been uncoupled from the sacramental life of the Church, when they were always meant to go together in order for us to experience the fullness of the spiritual life.

As Cardinal Sarah said:

> Prayer is the greatest need of the contemporary world; it remains the tool with which to reform the world. In an age that no longer prays, time is, so to speak, abolished, and life turns into a rat race.[302]

---

298 Bishop Milan Lach, SJ, "A Year of Renewal," Pastoral Letter to the Faithful of the Byzantine Catholic Eparchy of Parma, January 6, 2019. The Year 2019 is the 50th anniversary of the founding of the eparchy, and Bishop Milan called all of the faithful to a year of spiritual renewal.
299 Matthew Kelly, *Rediscover the Saints*, 118.
300 Hieromonk Maximos Davies, "Lenten Mission 2018: Hope," February 24, 2018.
301 See Gabriel Bunge, OSB, *Earthen Vessels*, 9.
302 Robert Cardinal Sarah, *God or Nothing*, 150.

A contemporary Athonite monk would concur, saying sacred silence (Hesychasm) is necessary for the renewal of the Church and for its pastoral work in the world.[303] He adds that perhaps the fruit of this renewal will be a greater desire to cultivate one's interior life,[304] that which we referred to earlier as inner monasticism.

Many people today are not grounded in the Good News of the Gospel and, as such, have not been formed by remaining with Christ, allowing him to lead, guide, and strengthen them. It is as if they need to be reintroduced to the Art of Spiritual Life. Accordingly, we begin with our vocation to holiness and then assist others (spiritual accompaniment). By uniting with others on the journey as members of the body of Christ, we also create the right environment in which faith can be nurtured, first within well-grounded families, and then within parish communities. We need our parishes to be beacons of light and hope amid the darkness. We need them to provide the necessary formation in the spiritual life so that we can achieve our vocation to holiness and help others to do so as well. Most importantly, we need our parishes to become true schools of prayer, creating the ability for people to have a genuine encounter with the Risen Christ, to open up avenues for people who are seeking to God to *experience* faith. St. John of Kronstadt reflected in his spiritual diary, "Prayer is a gold chain linking the Christian, a wanderer and stranger, with the spiritual world of which he is a member, and above all, with God, the Source of Life."[305] "Teaching people to pray is central to our mission as Christians," wrote Matthew Kelly. "If we do not teach people to pray, nothing will change. It is time for us to become a spiritual people again."[306] Finally, Cardinal Sarah warns, "A church that does not have prayer as its most precious treasure is headed for ruin."[307]

Complacency also is not something to be taken lightly. We have

303 See Monk Moses, *Athonite Flowers*, 45.
304 Ibid.
305 St. John of Kronstadt, *My Life in Christ*, Part 1, 76.
306 Matthew Kelly, *Rediscover the Saints*, 31.
307 Robert Cardinal Sarah, *The Day is Now Far Spent*, 16.

observed the cooling of faith in Western Europe. For example, in the Netherlands, more than two-thirds of the churches will be closed or sold by 2025,[308] with Dutch bishops fully acknowledging it was a failure to evangelize and seed the faith in subsequent generations after the Second Vatican Council. In North America, we are not immune; for example in September 2017, a panel for the Diocese of Pittsburgh proposed a "massive restructuring for merging its current 188 parishes into 48."[309] Reasons cited were the decline in the number of priests and decreases in church participation. Cardinal Sarah calls this "silent apostasy"[310]—we say nothing and do nothing as our faith gradually erodes and the government takes positions that are counter to traditional Church teaching.

It's up to us to continue the work of Pentecost and assist others on the journey. The urgency has never been greater. So, are we truly stewards of the treasures that have been passed on to us, often at great price? Are we truly willing to live our vocation to holiness at home and in our parish communities? As we contemplate our mission, consider the words of Elder Porphyrios:

> Living faith moves people, regenerates them and changes them, whereas words alone remain fruitless. The best form of mission is through our own example, our love and meekness.[311]

---

308 See Tom Heneghan, "Dutch Bishops Give Pope Francis a Bleak Picture of the Catholic Church in Decline," *FaithWorld* (Reuters Online, December 3, 2013).

309 Peter Smith, "Catholic Panel Recommends Parish Mergers," *Pittsburgh Post-Gazette* (Sept. 16, 2017).

310 See Fr. Gerald E. Murray, "Cardinal Sarah and Our Silent Apostasy," *The Catholic Thing* (Jan. 16, 2016). "The root problem in Western society—and the Church—comes down to this: degrees of unbelief in God and in his revelation. This unbelief ranges from atheism (theoretical and practical) to agnosticism (often the fruit of ignorance, laziness, or spiritual blindness) to pick-and-choose Catholicism. When we fail to adhere unreservedly to Christ and his teaching, we are left to our own devices—not a happy thought. Sarah states: 'If the tie between God and Christians is weakened, the Church becomes simply a human structure, one society among others. With that, the Church becomes trivial; she makes herself worldly and is corrupted to the point of losing her original nature. Indeed, without God we create a Church in our own image, for our little needs, likes, and dislikes.'"

311 Elder Porphyrios, *Wounded by Love*, 187.

We are called to be Jesus's witnesses to all the nations.[312] Through our vocation to holiness, we begin by demonstrating in the way we live what we deem important to us. As Christians, we are called to go into the world, but not to be the world or to be swept away by it.[313] Further, we discern what we as a community can do to bring the Gospel message to those who have fallen away, the disenfranchised, and the unchurched. We are called to pass on the gift of faith entrusted to us by previous generations. However, as St. Basil the Great (330-379) would tell us, we cannot give what we ourselves do not have.[314] So, we must be first grounded and formed in our faith. In turn, we come together as "a community of missionary disciples" to share Christ with others, to be his light in the midst of darkness and authentic witnesses to the Good News of the Gospel. As Pope Benedict XVI wrote, "What the world is in particular need of today is the credible witness of people … capable of opening the hearts and minds of many to the desire for God and for true life."[315] We need to be counter-cultural, lifting the world up. Christ is the only source of life. Without Christ, we will have no life within us.

Reflection for Conference No. 4 (Option 1)

> Today the West lives as if God did not exist. How could countries with ancient Christian and spiritual traditions cut themselves off from their roots to such an extent? The consequences appear to be so tragic that it is essential to understand the origin of this phenomenon.

---

312 See Matt. 28:16-20. The Great Commissioning.

313 See Pronechen, "Archbishop Sheen's Warning of a Crisis in Christendom," 3.

314 See Joseph J. Allen, *The Ministry of the Church: The Image of Pastoral Care* (Crestwood, NY: St. Vladimir's Seminary Press: 1986), 144-145. Basil the Great, *Moral Rule 70*: "The leader must himself possess what he brings. One must not put constraint upon others to do what he has not done himself. The leader of the word should make himself an example to others of every good thing, practicing first what he teaches."

315 Pope Benedict XVI, *Porta Fidei* (Rome: Libreria Editrice Vaticana, 2011), no. 15. This letter announced the Year of Faith, from October 11, 2012 to November 24, 2013. It should be noted that Pope Francis released his Apostolic Exhortation, *Evangelii Gaudium*, on November 24, 2013 to coincide with the conclusion of the Year of Faith.

The West decided to distance itself from the Christian faith under the influence of the Enlightenment philosophers and the resulting political currents. Although Christian communities exist that are still vital and missionary, most Western populations now regard Jesus as a sort of idea but not as an event, much less a person whom the apostles and many witnesses of the Gospel met and loved and to whom they consecrated their whole life.

This estrangement from God is not caused by reasoning but by a wish to be detached from him. The atheistic orientation of life is almost always a decision by the will. Man no longer wishes to reflect on his relationship with God because he himself intends to become God. His model is Prometheus, the mythological character of the race of Titans who stole sacred fire so as to give it to men; the individual has embarked on a strategy of appropriating God instead of adoring him. Before the so-called "Enlightenment" movement, if a man ever tried to take God's place, to be his equal, or to eliminate him, these were isolated individual phenomena.

Robert Cardinal Sarah with Nicolas Diat. *God or Nothing: A Conversation on Faith*. Translated by Michael J. Miller, 167-168. San Francisco, CA: Ignatius Press, 2015.

Reflection for Conference No. 4 (Option 2)

Of course, our world today is caught up in the same question that Pilate derisively asked Jesus: "Truth? What does that mean?" It has become virtually the definition of modernity to deny that permanent, objective truth exists apart from opinion. Everything is relative. No objective reality exists apart from our own perceptions and interpretations. Yet the statement of Jesus is clear: "For this was I born, and for this I have come into the world, to bear witness to the truth. Everyone who is of the truth hears my voice" (John 18:37). What the Church has taught consistently and always, is that the truth exists apart from us. It exists, whether we believe it or not. The eighth commandment tells us that we must find that truth in Jesus, we speak that truth in Jesus, and we must spread that truth in his name.

Archbishop Charles J. Chaput, OFM Cap. *Living the Catholic Faith: Rediscovering the Basics*, 105. Cincinnati, OH: St. Anthony Messenger Press, 2001.

Reflection Questions

1. How important is my faith to me? Please explain your answer.

2. Is my faith built on a foundation of rock or sand? How do I react in times of trial or crisis?

3. How do I share my faith with others? Does the way I live my life bear witness to my faith? At home? At work? When at church?

4. How do I feel about the importance of sharing my faith with others? Please explain your answer.

Icon of Christ the True Vine.

Christ is the true source of life. He tells us, "I am the true vine" (John 15:1); he tells his disciples that they are the branches (15:5); that a branch on its own cannot bear fruit (cf. 15:4); and without him they can do nothing (cf. 15:5). We need to remain connected to Christ in order to achieve eternal blessedness. Without Christ, we have no life within us (cf. 1 John 15:12). Self-reliance is a barren faith.

As St. John Kronstadt wrote in his spiritual diary: "The tree firmly fixed into the earth by its roots grows and brings forth fruit. The soul of the man firmly fixed in God through faith and love, like spiritual roots, also lives, grows spiritually, and produces the fruits of God, pleasing virtue, through which the soul lives now and shall live in the world to come. The tree, when uprooted from the ground, ceases to live the life it received from the soil through the roots. Similarly, the soul of a man who has lost faith and love for God and does not dwell in God, in whom alone he can live, spiritually dies. God is fertile earth for the soul."[316] Encounter and formation are intended to keep us rooted in God, allowing us to undergo gradual transformation and greater purification of the heart (*theosis*) in order to prepare us for eternal blessedness, sharing in the life of the Holy Trinity in the world to come.

The icon of Christ as the True Vine also reminds us of how we are all connected to Christ and to one another (one Body in Christ)—see Rom. 12:5.

---

316 St. John of Kronstadt, *My Life in Christ*, Part 1, 44.

CONCLUSION

Holiness

"Holiness befits your house, Lord, for all the length of days."
(Psalm 93:5)
"Lord! I am your vessel: fill me with the gifts of the Holy
Spirit. Without you, I am void of every blessing." [317]
(St. John of Kronstadt)

A Vocation to Holiness

Through the course of this retreat, we have reflected on a Vocation to Holiness, choosing the way of Christ over that of the secular world. As we conclude, let us consider some final questions. First, what is holiness? To answer, let us consider the thoughts of St. John of Kronstadt:

> What is holiness? It is freedom from every sin and fullness of virtue. This freedom from sin and this virtuous life are only attainted by a few zealous persons, not immediately, but gradually, through prolonged and manifold sorrows, sicknesses, and labors, through fasting, vigilance, prayer, not by their own strength, but by the grace of Christ.[318]

---

317 St. John of Kronstadt, *My Life in Christ*, Part 2, 149.
318 Ibid., 26.

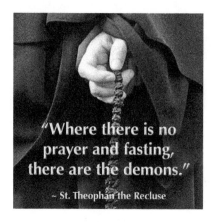

"Where there is no prayer and fasting, there are the demons."

~ St. Theophan the Recluse

This is a good summary of our retreat reflections. It reemphasizes that this is about entering through the narrow gate; that it requires patience, struggle, and perseverance; that we need ascetical practices and prayer; and that alone, it is impossible to achieve. As Jesus told his disciples after the rich young man turned and walked away, having heard the terms of following Jesus and the means of becoming perfect, "For human beings this is impossible, but for God all things are possible."[319] Therein lies a critical message. Our salvation requires Divine – human collaboration, or *synergeia*. As St. John or Kronstadt tells us, "You see very clearly that it is extremely difficult for you to change for the better. In fact, without God's grace and your own fervent prayer and abstinence, it would be impossible."[320] Further, we are free to make the choice to follow Jesus or not, and God will respect our opinion. He gave us free will, wherein surrender of self-will to the Divine-will is completely our own choice. Consider the rich young man who walked away. Jesus respected his decision.

Nowhere in the Gospel is the road to eternal blessedness considered easy. Quite the contrary. Jesus's way is the Way of the Cross ("If anyone wishes to come after me, he must deny himself and take up his cross daily and follow me."[321]). It is about step-by-step incremental transformation, constantly working at a life of virtue and avoiding the snares of the demons. All the Spiritual Fathers and Mothers tell us that it is a struggle and it is easy to stumble along the way, to be overcome by temptation, especially when it means following the crowd, giving into the messages of secular society. It is so hard to give up the tempting fruit, even when Jesus stretches out

---

319 Matt. 19:26.
320 St. John of Kronstadt, *My Life in Christ*, Part 2, 37.
321 Luke 9:23.

his hand to guide us, saying, "Come, follow me. I am the way." How hard it is to surrender to God's will for our lives. That is why many try to compromise, to find an easier way, to widen the narrow gate, or to compromise with the spirit of the age. With all the allure of earthly splendor, riches, and honors, we face a significant challenge of self-surrender.

> Unfortunately, we have little faith in Christ, and we try to combine our love for the world with love for Christ, to unite earthly attachments with love for God. These things are incompatible! *"If anyone desires to come after me, let him deny himself"* (Matt. 16:24) of everything is passionately attached to in the world, and let him hate his own sin-loving soul.[322]

As we discussed throughout the retreat, there are only two ways. There is no middle way. For us to achieve eternal blessedness in the life to come, we need to listen to the invitation of Jesus: "Be with me. Let me lead you, guide you, teach you. Let me give you strength. Surrender yourself to me and I will take care of everything." We need to love God with our whole soul, not just part of it.[323] It is an all-in commitment.

This brings us to the second important question as we near the end of this retreat. If our vocation to holiness begins with following Jesus and this is an all-in commitment, who is Jesus to me? Each of us must answer this question for ourselves. Some in society today want to marginalize the importance of Jesus, diminishing him to solely a historical figure or an ideal. Yet if we accept this perspective, we are in fact denying the divinity of Jesus. The Risen Jesus is alive and desires to dwell in our hearts. He will show us the way to the Father.

---

322 Ibid., 101. The date of this diary entry is December 24, 1869.
323 St. John of Kronstadt regularly writes in his spiritual journal, "The soul is simple and indivisible." We cannot serve two masters. As an example see *My Life in Christ*, Part 2, 142.

We said that Jesus is meant to be experienced, that we enter into genuine relationship with him who desires a genuine relationship with us. One cannot have a relationship with a deceased historical figure from 2,000 years ago or an ideal, much less love him. So, who is Jesus to me? The answer to this question is key to our decision to pursue a vocation to holiness, because Jesus is the foundation.

Returning to the Four Fundamental Questions

This brings us back to the four fundamental questions from our Introduction, which we asked each participant to consider throughout this retreat. While each individual must answer the questions for him- or herself, we can provide some perspectives.

1. Who is Jesus Christ?

> Jesus is not just a historical figure or an ideal. He is the Incarnate Son of the Living God. "For God so loved the world that he gave his only Son, so that everyone who believes in him might not perish but might have eternal life."[324] This is the context in which we have presented Jesus throughout this retreat, as the Son of God and the Word of God. The Incarnation of Jesus is a historical event, which makes it both irrevocable and irreversible because God himself has acted in the world.[325] Jesus is God's gift to us, a personalized invitation to eternal blessedness. In essence, God gives himself to us.

> So who is Jesus? We would propose the following for consideration[326]:

---

324 John 3:16.
325 See Edward Kleinguetl, *Encounter: Experiencing the Divine Presence* (Parker CO: Outskirts Press, 2018), 60. This concept draws upon the theological framework of Karl Rahner, SJ (1904-84), one of the foremost Catholic theologians of the twentieth century.
326 Ibid., 65.

Jesus is	God	*Jesus is consubstantial with the Father (same essence)*
		• "In the beginning was the Word, and the word was with God, and the Word was God" (John 1:1). • "The Father and I are one" (John 10:30). • "Image of the invisible God" (Col. 1:15). • "In these last days, (God) spoke to us through a Son" (see Heb. 1:2).
	Gift	*Jesus is God's gift to humanity*
		• "For God so loved the world that he gave his only Son, so that everyone who believes in him might not perish but might have eternal life" (John 3:16). Jesus is God's personal invitation, given in love to humanity, to share in eternal blessedness. • "I came so that they might have life and have it more abundantly" (John 10:10).
	Our Model (Guide)	*Jesus is our example of how to accept God's gift*
		• Jesus, though he was in the form of God, did not regard equality with God, something to be grasped. Rather, he emptied self, taking the form of a slave" (Phil. 2:6-7). • "I am the way and the truth and the life" (John 14:6). • "If anyone wishes to come after me, he must deny himself and take up his cross daily and follow me" (Luke 9:23). • "I have given you a model to follow, so that as I have done for you, you should also do" (John 13:5). Jesus washed the feet of disciples, the role of a slave. • "Not my will but yours be done" (Luke 22:42); surrender of self-will to the Divine-will. • "Father, forgive them, they know not what they do" (Luke 23:34). • "Father, into your hands I commend my spirit" (Luke 23:46). • Jesus led a life of humility, obedience, and patient endurance (see Conference No. 3).
	Our Goal	*Jesus is "divinized humanity"*[326]
		• "We will...make our dwelling with him" (John 14:23). • "Remain in me, as I remain in you" (John 15:4). • "I am the vine, you are the branches. Whoever remains in me and I in him will bear much fruit, because without me you can do nothing" (John 15:5). • "Whoever acknowledges that Jesus is the Son of God, God remains in him and he in God" (1 John 4:15). • "You may come to share in the divine nature" (2 Pet. 1:4).

---

327 Divinized Humanity" – At the Council of Chalcedon in 451, Jesus was proclaimed to be fully human and fully divine: "Truly God and truly man...two natures without confusion, without change, without division, without separation." Our destiny as human beings is union with God, "sharers in the divine nature" (2 Pet. 1:4), but we do not become part of the divine nature. Rather, humanity and divinity while living in union, remain distinct in essence. Thus, the Incarnation Son of God represents our goal, the union of Divine and human.

While each person must decide who Jesus is for him or her personally, the above is worthy of our consideration and, at least for us, provides the compelling reason of why to say "yes" to Jesus's call. It is the only way to achieve eternal blessedness (see Conference No. 1). As St. Paul wrote: "

Do not conform yourselves to this age but be transformed by the renewal of your mind, that you may discern what is the will of God, what is good and pleasing and perfect.[328]

2. How do we come to know and love Jesus Christ?

Jesus is meant to be experienced. During this retreat, we specifically discussed prayer as a means of encountering Jesus. This is an important means of cultivating our spiritual life, more precisely, a personal relationship with Christ. However, prayer cannot be separated from the sacramental life of the Church, especially the Holy Mysteries of Repentance and Eucharist. We also encounter Jesus in the liturgy. We come to know Jesus through the Sacred Scriptures, especially the Gospels. In essence, this was our discussion about encounter (Conference No. 2).

3. How does Jesus Christ teach us to live a good and moral life?

The Gospel provides us with the teachings and examples of Jesus. The rest of the New Testament illustrates how in apostolic times, people followed Jesus, living the way he taught. Similarly, our Church Fathers and Mothers throughout the ages have provided us witness by their lives and writings as to how they lived as disciples of Jesus. In essence, this is how we allow Jesus to form us, which in turn leads to personal transformation, our incremental conversion to become more Christ-like (*theosis*) in preparation for our destiny: union with God. See Conference No. 3.

---

328 Rom. 12:2.

4. **How are we called to become missionary disciples of Jesus Christ?**

As followers of Jesus, we are entrusted with the same mission originally given to the apostles: "Go ... and make disciples of all nations, baptizing them in the name of the Father, and of the Son, and of the Holy Spirit, teaching them to observe all that I have commanded you."[329] We are entrusted with the deposit of faith, to be passed on to the next generation, just as it has been since the time of the apostles. Thus, we follow the Christian way of life, gather in communities to create an environment conducive to growth and ongoing conversion (transformation), and bear witness to a fallen world.

Going Forth

As we leave our retreat, we must each choose the way we will go: Life in Christ, or the way of the secular world. One leads to eternal life, the other to despair, hopelessness, and death. Should we choose the former, we must also realize it is a daily commitment, of struggling and remaining ever vigilant. Consider the words of St. Paul in his letter to the Philippians.

Closing Reading

Read: Phil. 3:17-20 (Our Goal).

Join with others in being imitators of me, brothers, and observe those who thus conduct themselves according to the model you have in us.

For many, as I have often told you and now tell you

---

329 Matt. 28:19-20.

even in tears, conduct themselves as enemies of the cross of Christ.

Their end is destruction. Their God is their stomach; their glory is in their "shame." Their minds are occupied with earthly things.

But our citizenship is in heaven, and from it we also await a savior, the Lord Jesus Christ.[330]

---

330 Phil. 3:16-20.

Icon of the Mandylion (Holy Napkin). The Mandylion was a holy relic consisting of a piece of cloth upon which the image of the face of Jesus Christ had been miraculously imprinted without human intervention. Some associate it with the veil by which Veronica wiped the face of Jesus. (Icon written by the hand of Subdeacon Miron Kerul-Kmec, Jr.)

Our vocation to holiness prepares us for our destiny, eternal blessedness in heaven and union with God. This involves a constant effort to cultivate and increasingly exhibit the attributes of God as modeled by Jesus: goodness, love, mercy, compassion, longsuffering, patience, purity, and having pure love for neighbor. It is a lifelong journey of transformation that can only be accomplished through Divine collaboration (*synergeia*). "For human beings this is impossible, but for God all things are possible" (Matt. 19:26).

Evangelization

"Here I am... Send me!"
(Isa. 6:8)

*"I would like all of us to ask ourselves today: Are we
still a Church capable of warming hearts?"*[331]
(Pope Francis)

*"At its root, the crisis through which the clergy, the Church, and
the world are going is a spiritual crisis, a crisis of faith."*[332]
(Robert Cardinal Sarah)

Introduction to the Post-Retreat Discussion

During our retreat, we focused on our vocation to holiness, saying "yes" to Jesus, allowing him to lead us, guide us, and teach us; to give us strength. Through our encounters with Jesus and being formed by him, we are transformed, drawing ever closer to eternal blessedness, which is sharing in the life of the Holy Trinity. This transformation is first individual (the foundation), and second in our communities (spiritual accompaniment). In turn, our transformed communities provide evangelical witness, healing, and the lifting up of our broken world. We become the light of Christ shining in the midst of a world shrouded in darkness. And, the world desperately needs our light.

In the introduction to this of the retreat, one of the four questions we were asked to reflect upon is: "How are we called to be missionary disciples of Jesus Christ?" As a true disciple of Christ, we

---

331 Pope Francis, Address to the Meeting of the Bishops of Brazil (July 28, 2013), Sec. 3. This address was made on the eve of World Youth Day in Rio de Janeiro.
332 Robert Cardinal Sarah, *The Day is Now Far Spent*, 12.

are responsible for fulfilling Jesus's commandment to share the Good News of the Gospel. As members of the body of Christ, we have a responsibility for one another. Pope St. John Paul II wrote in terms of the New Evangelization, saying, "Those who have come into genuine contact with Christ cannot keep him for themselves; they must proclaim him."[333] With that in mind, let us reflect on our ongoing responsibilities of discipleship.

Opening Gospel Passage

Read: Matt. 28:16-20 (The Commissioning of the Disciples).

Reexamining the Call to Discipleship

By virtue of our Baptism and desire to pursue our vocation to holiness, we are called to be missionary disciples, which necessarily means becoming evangelists. However, "to become evangelizers, we must first be evangelized."[334] Our evangelization comes through saying "yes" to Jesus and remaining committed to the path of holiness. We must keep ourselves united To God. It is a real priority to find time to pray and receive Holy Eucharist. Prayer gives life to the ministry.[335] Thus, through our focus on the interior life, we prepare ourselves for prophetic witness and action.[336]

In his seminal work, *Evangelii Nuntiandi*, Pope Paul VI wrote, "Above all the Gospel must be proclaimed by witness."[337] Faith is like a fire. A person must be on fire in order to transmit faith.[338] As disciples, do those around us notice a discernible difference in the way we live

---

333 Pope John Paul II, *Novo Millennio Ineunte* (Rome: Libreria Editrice Vaticana, Jan. 6, 2001), no. 40.
334 United States Catholic Conference of Bishops, Committee on Evangelization and Catechesis, *Disciples Called to Witness: The New Evangelization* (January 20, 2013), 21.
335 See Robert Cardinal Sarah, *The Day is Now Far Spent*, 55.
336 See Monk Moses, *Athonite Flowers*, 45.
337 Pope Paul VI, *Evangelii Nuntiandi*, no. 21.
338 See Robert Cardinal Sarah, *The Day is Now Far Spent*, 222.

our lives, in our priorities, in our love and compassion for others, and as people who believe in hope in adversity? Today, through witness, we will stand in stark contrast to the prominent culture and, arguably, our world needs this reminder of Gospel values through our personal witness. This means more than a testimonial or words; rather, it is manifested through our actions. Pope Paul VI wrote:

> Those who sincerely accept the Good News, through the power of this acceptance and of shared faith therefore gather together in Jesus's name in order to seek together the kingdom, build it up and live it. They make up a community which is in its turn evangelizing.[339]

So, by saying "yes" to Jesus, through our vocation to holiness, we contribute to the body of Christ. Further, through divine collaboration (*synergeia*), it is the gentle breezes of the Holy Spirit that has the power to open doors and windows of the hearts of people.[340] However to become that evangelizing community, we begin with our individual commitment.

> The New Evangelization is a call to each person to deepen his or her faith, have confidence in the Gospel, and possess a willingness to share the Gospel. It is a personal *encounter* with the person of Jesus, which brings joy and peace. The New Evangelization provides the lens through which people experience the Church and world around them.[341]

Again, the catalyst for evangelization is personal witness. Consider the example of Caitlin. She was baptized Catholic and was going

---

339 Pope Paul VI, *Evangelii Nuntiandi*, no. 13.
340 See Monk Moses, *Athonite Flowers*, 45.
341 United States Catholic Conference of Bishops, *Disciples Called to Witness*, 3. Emphasis added by the author.

through the motions until high school. By college, she had almost completely drifted away from the Church. Later, she was married, struggled with a number of issues, and found herself in a session of Catholics Returning Home. When asked why she came that evening, her first words were, "I want what my husband has." His view of life was much more optimistic, she said, well-grounded in his Catholic faith and drawing strength from it. That's what she wanted too! Do our lives bear witness to our faith? Do people want what we have?

As St. Basil the Great reminded us, we cannot give what we ourselves do not have. We need to be formed by Christ, to have encountered him, and said "yes" to following him, and cultivating a deeper relationship with him. As Cardinal Sarah writes:

> The chief preoccupation of all disciples of Jesus must be their sanctification. The first place in their lives must be given to prayer, to silent contemplation, and to the Eucharist, without which all the rest would be vain agitation.[342]

Further, we cannot escape the fact that following Christ also means taking up our cross daily.[343] As Cardinal Sarah tells us, we must make the Cross central again. "We do not have to make the Church acceptable according to the world's criteria. We have to purify her so that she presents to the world the Cross in all its nakedness."[344] Do we in our lives authentically represent the Gospel of Jesus Christ, that his way is the Way of the Cross? In our introduction, we referenced Tertullian and that witness borne through sacrifice provides the seed for conversion. While today that sacrifice may not involve spilling blood (at least in our country), it may involve the willingness to stand in radical opposition to the prevailing cultural winds. Consider the reflections of German Pastor and Theologian Dietrich Bonhoeffer

---

342 Robert Cardinal Sarah, *The Day is Now Far Spent*, 30.
343 See Luke 9:23.
344 Robert Cardinal Sarah, *The Day is Now Far Spent*, 36.

(1906-1945), in his comparison of cheap grace versus costly grace:

> Cheap grace is the preaching of forgiveness without repentance, baptism without church discipline, Communion without confession, absolution without personal confession. Cheap grace is grace without discipleship, grace without the cross, grace without Jesus Christ, living and incarnate.[345]

This is the way the world tries to mold Christianity today, to accommodate the spirit of the age, trying to widen the narrow gate, and to eliminate the Cross. Thus, it tries to devalue the importance of the Gospel of Jesus Christ. To this, Bonhoeffer provides a contrast:

> Costly grace is the gospel which must be *sought* again and again, the gift which must be *asked for*, the door at which a man must *knock*. Such grace is *costly* because it causes us to follow, and it is *grace* because it call us to follow *Jesus Christ*. It is costly because it costs a man his life, and it is grace because it gives a man the only true life. It is costly because it condemns sin, and grace because it justifies the sinner. Above all, it is *costly* because it cost God the life of his Son.[346]

True faith has a price and it must be lived authentically, staying the course and not trying to seek a non-existent easier way. There is no other way except the way of the Cross, through which Jesus restored our relationship with God and invites us into eternal blessedness, union with God. This is how we as Christians truly provide witness to a broken world. As Cardinal Sarah writes, "Faith is contagious. If it is not, that is because it has become insipid."[347]

---

345 Dietrich Bonhoeffer, *The Cost of Discipleship* (New York: Simon & Schuster, 1995), 44-45.
346 Ibid., 45.
347 Robert Cardinal Sarah, *The Day is Now Far Spent*, 25.

Throughout the retreat, we spoke of the choice between the way of Jesus and the way of the dominant culture, and that there is no middle way. If we choose the former, the vocation to holiness, it is an "all in" decision including compassion and concern for our neighbor. We are bound together by love of Christ, to love those whom Christ loves (i.e., all people) and, in turn, we take on a responsibility for evangelization, primarily through personal witness reflected in the life we lead. We are entrusted with the mission that Jesus gave to his disciples before the Ascension and reinforced through the Pentecost event, wherein the Church was formed. Jesus said, "I have come to set a fire on the earth, and how I wish it were already blazing!"[348] Our witness perpetuates that fire, which sustains the efforts of evangelization. It is how we truly become a community of missionary disciples, lifting up a world in need of healing.[349] As Pope Francis writes in *Evangelii Gaudium*, in a paragraph specifically referencing Mother Teresa of Calcutta, "An authentic faith—which is never comfortable or completely personal—always involves a deep desire to change the world ..."[350]

A truly beautiful church is not one with incredible artistry or marble or gold. True beauty is a church in which its members have hearts ablaze with love for Jesus.[351] It is a place where true zeal and energy can be experienced. "The pure heart is most beautiful temple of God."[352] Would that people say about us, "We want what they have!"

Reflection from St. John Chrysostom (349-407)

You are the salt of the earth. It is not for your own sake, he says, but for the world's sake that the word

---

348 Luke 12:49.
349 See also Paul VI, *Evangelii Nuntiandi*, no. 13.
350 Pope Francis, *Evangelii Gaudium*, no. 183.
351 See Luke 24:32.
352 Robert Cardinal Sarah, *The Day is Now Far Spent*, 238.

is entrusted to you. I am not sending you into two cities or ten or twenty, not to a single nation, as I sent the prophets of old, but across land and sea, to the whole world. And that world is in a miserable state. For when he says: *You are the salt of the earth*, he is indicating that all mankind had lost its savor and had been corrupted by sin. Therefore, he requires of these men those virtues which are especially useful and even necessary if they are to bear the burdens of many. For the man who is kindly, modest, merciful, and just will not keep his good works to himself, but will see to it that these admirable fountains send out their streams for the good of others. Again, the man who is clean of heart, a peacemaker and ardent for truth will order his life so as to contribute to the common good.

Do not think he says, that you are destined for easy struggles or unimportant tasks. *You are the salt of the earth*. What do these words imply? Did the disciples restore what had already turned rotten? Not at all. Salt cannot help what is already corrupted. That is not what they did. But what had first been renewed and freed from corruption and turned over to them, they salted and preserved in the newness the Lord had bestowed. It took the power of Christ to free men from the corruption caused by sin; it was the task of the apostles through strenuous labor to keep that corruption from returning.

If others lose their savor, then your ministry will help them regain it. But if you yourselves suffer that loss, you will drag others down with you. Therefore, the greater the undertakings put into your hands, the more zealous you must be. For this reason he says: *But if the salt becomes tasteless, how can its flavor be restored?*

It is good for nothing now, but to be thrown out and trampled by men's feet.

When they hear the words: *When they curse you and persecute you and accuse you of every evil,* they may be afraid to come forward. Therefore he says: "Unless you are prepared for that sort of thing, it is in vain that I have chosen you. Curses shall necessarily be your lot, but they shall not harm you and will simply be a testimony to your constancy. If through fear, however, you fail to show the forcefulness your mission demands, your lot will be much worse, for all will speak evil of you and despise you. That is what being trampled by men's feet means."

Then he passes on to a more exalted comparison: *You are the light of the world.* Once again, "of the world": not of one nation or twenty cities, but of the whole world. The light he means is an intelligible light, far superior to the rays of the sun we see, just as salt is spiritual salt. First salt, then light, so that you may learn how profitable sharp words may be how useful serious doctrine. Such teaching holds in check and prevents dissipation; it leads to virtue and sharpen the mind's eye. *A city set on a hill cannot be hidden, nor do men light a lamp and put it under a basket.* Here again he is urging them to a careful manner of life and teaching them to be watchful, for they live under the eyes of all and have the whole world for the arena of their struggles.

St. John Chrysostom. Homily on "Matthew No. 15." Taken from *The Liturgy of the Hours,* vol. IV, 120-122. New York: Catholic Book Publishing Co., 1975.

Alternative Reflection from Pope Francis: "What does the Church Need Today?"

A martyr can be thought of as a hero, but the fundamental thing about a martyr is that he or she was graced: it is the grace of God, not courage, that makes us martyrs.... "What does the Church need today?" Martyrs, witnesses, namely everyday saints, because the Church is led by saints. Saints: without them, the Church can no longer go forth. The Church needs everyday saints, those of ordinary life carried out with coherence; but she also needs those who ... accept grace to be witnesses to the end, unto death. All those are the living blood of the Church. They are the witnesses ... who attest that Jesus is risen, that Jesus lives, and affirm it with coherence of life and with the strength of the Holy Spirit which they have been given.

Pope Francis. Homily at Holy Mass in memory of the martyrs of the 20th and 21st centuries. Rome: Libreria Editrice Vaticana (April 22, 2007). Taken from "The Grace that Overcomes Duplicity," *Magnificat*, 21, no. 6 (2019): 354-355.

Alternative Reflection: "The Church on Mission"

Neutrality is not possible. Faced with the hope of a real diminishment and vanquishing of evil, no one can be neutral, because, as Jesus says, *"Whoever is not with me is against me, and whoever does not gather with me scatters"* (Matt. 12:30; Luke 11:23). In our commitment to make the kingdom of God present, therefore, we must make the decision to be on the side of Jesus, to gather with him; because not to do good in the way of Jesus means that one is already allowing, in a certain sense, evil. There are no definitive states in the fight against evil except in the paschal victory of Jesus over death ....

The missionary disciple must, like Jesus, be involved in the struggle against evil. This should be one of our main concerns, because it genuinely demonstrates our filial relationship with God and our communion with Jesus. Curiously, however, being witnesses demands that disciples confront their humanity. On the one hand, they must be aware of being able, by virtue of grace and effort, to participate in the Lord's mission. But along with these great possibilities, disciples must also be aware of their limitations .... It is being with Jesus, belonging to him, that determines and supports our struggle against every form of evil.

"The Church on Mission," *Magnificat*, 21, no. 8 (2019): 174.

Reflection Questions

1. Does my life bear witness to Jesus? Are my priorities his priorities? Or am I a different person at home, at work, and at church? How deep is my relationship with Christ?

2. How can I bring the light of Christ to a darkened world? What talents do I have that I use for Christ?

3. How can I lift up my community and how can my community lift up the world?

Icon of Christ Commissioning the Apostles.

Jesus commissioned his disciples to go out to the whole world, announcing the Good News of the Gospel (see Matt. 28:19). Since that time, the faith has been transmitted through the generations to us today. In many cases, this treasure was preserved at great cost during persecution and trial. Consider in modern times, for example, the Cristero Rebellion in Mexico in the 1920s, Nazism, Communism, and Socialism during the 20th century, repression during the Cultural Revolution in China, or the persecution of Christians in Africa and Middle East today. Many of our ancestors paid a great price to give us what we have today. Now, we are entrusted with passing on our deposit of faith to the next generation. Are we willing to be good stewards of that which has been entrusted to us? Are we willing to stand in radical opposition to the prevailing culture, authentically bearing witness to the Gospel of Jesus Christ? How we live our faith makes it relevant to others.

Choosing Life in Christ

"In the early Church, Christians were called the 'saints' because their whole lives were imbued with the presence of Christ and with the light of his Gospel. They were in the minority, but they transformed the world. Christ never promised his faithful that they would be in the majority."[353]

As Christians, we must live up to our vocation to holiness. As Pope Leo the Great said, "Christian, know your dignity!" To this, Cardinal Sarah would advise: "Do not deprive yourself of the treasure of the faith."[354]

353 Robert Cardinal Sarah, *The Day is Now Far Spent*, 30.
354 Ibid., 320-321.

Pivotal Players

The following are some of the individuals referenced in our conferences.

Basil the Great, St. (330-79) – also known as Basil of Caesarea. Bishop and influential theologian who supported the Nicaean Creed. He is considered one of the three Cappadocian Fathers, along with his brother, St. Gregory of Nyssa, and St. Gregory the Theologian (Nazianzus), who did much to develop Trinitarian doctrine.

Chaput, Charles J., OFM Cap. (1945—) – Archbishop of Philadelphia, installed in 2011. Previously Archbishop of Denver (1997-2011) and Bishop of Rapid City (1988-1997). He is a professed Franciscan Capuchin, and a member of the Prairie Band Potawatomi Nation, the second Native American bishop and first archbishop. A significant portion of his teaching is on evangelization. His books include *Living the Catholic Faith: Rediscovering the Basics* (2001) and *Strangers in a Strange Land: Practicing the Catholic Faith in a Post-Christian World* (2017).

Chrysostom, St. John (c. 349-407) – a prolific homilist and pastoral theologian. Originally from Antioch, he was first an ascetic, later a priest, and then elected as Archbishop of Constantinople in 397. Many of his homilies and writings are available to us today. He is particularly known for his teachings on wealth and poverty. In addition, he is associated with the most-used liturgical form in the Eastern Churches, the Divine Liturgy of St. John Chrysostom.

Climacus, St. John (579-649) – a monk and later abbot of St. Catherine's Monastery on Mt. Sinai. His most notable work is *The Ladder of Divine Ascent*, which describes the ascetical and spiritual practices for raising one's self up to God. He describes each practice as one of 30 steps, using the analogy of Jacob's ladder (see Gen. 28:12) for his spiritual teaching and the number of steps being the age of Jesus at his baptism. It is the most translated book in Christianity behind the Bible and liturgical books.

Desert Fathers and Mothers – early Christians who went in the desert between the third and seventh centuries, initially in Egypt and later in Palestine and Syria. Their desire was to follow the example of Jesus, withdrawing into the desert and encountering God in solitude. Theirs was a "back-to-basics" spirituality. The wisdom of these desert dwellers is simple, and the collection of these sayings is referred to as the *Apophthegmata Patrum* ("Sayings of the Fathers"). Some of the more significant Desert Fathers are:

- Abba Agathon (ca. fourth century).

- Abba Arsenius (ca. 350–445).

- Dorotheos of Gaza (505–65), Syrian Desert.

- Abba Isaiah the Solitary (d. 491).

- St. John Climacus (c.579-649), Mt. Sinai.

- Abba John the Dwarf (ca. 339–405).

- Abba Macarius the Great (c. 300-91).

- Abba Moses the Black (or Moses the Ethiopian) (330–405).

- Abba Pachomius (292-348).

- Abba Poemen (d. 450).

The sayings of all these Desert Fathers — except Dorotheos of Gaza and St. John Climacus, who were later —can be found in *The Sayings of the Desert Fathers*. Dorotheos of Gaza's wisdom is included in *Discourses and Sayings*. St. John Climacus wrote the classic, *The*

Ladder of Divine Ascent (see above). The lessons of these Desert Dwellers are particularly relevant to our time as they represent a back-to-basics spirituality, reflective of the fact that the Church is ever ancient, ever new. In a time when people desire things that are organic, original, without additives, or preservatives, the lessons of the Desert Fathers and Mothers are worth considering in terms of essential fundamentals of faith.

Francis, Pope (1936–) – elected to the papacy on March 13, 2013. Born Jorge Maria Bergoglio in Argentina, he was previously the Cardinal Archbishop of Buenos Aires. He is the first Jesuit Pope. His Apostolic Exhortation, *Evangelii Gaudium* (November 24, 2013), essentially provides an overview of a spiritual theology of encounter.

Gregory of Nyssa, St. (c. 335–95) – one of the three Cappadocian Fathers, all three of whom were bishops, and included St. Basil the Great (his brother) and St. Gregory the Theologian. He was one of the Early Greek Fathers who first discussed the concept of *theosis* but rarely used the actual term. He also made significant contributions to the doctrine of the Trinity and to the Nicaean Creed. In the movement known as *ressourcement* (a return to the sources), theologians prior to and leading up to the Second Vatican Council began to consider the perspectives of these Early Church Fathers within their own theological frameworks. Thus, one finds similarities between theologians like St. Gregory of Nyssa of the Early Church and modern theologians such as Karl Rahner, SJ, one of the most influential Catholic theologians of the twentieth century.

Isaac the Syrian, St. (640-700) – a later Desert Father, originally from Qatar, he was later the Bishop of Nineveh (modern-day Baghdad). He is best known for his works on asceticism and is revered by monks, especially those from the Christian East. Elder Joseph the Hesychast from Mt. Athos (1897-1959) advised that if one could only have a single book, it should be *The Ascetical Homilies of Saint Isaac the Syrian*. Elder Paisios of Mount Athos (1924-94) taught, "You can read just one sentence of Abba Isaac, and it's got enough spiritual vitamins to last for a week or a month." Further, he called books like of Isaac the Syrian "meaty," and he is right. The writings of Abba Isaac are so rich with meaning that they need to be savored in small increments, to be reflected upon, given the depth of meaning contained therein.

John of Kronstadt, St. (1829-1908) – was a Russian Orthodox priest and spiritual director serving St. Andrew's Cathedral in Kronstadt, a naval base and penal colony near St. Petersburg. Living in circumstances of extreme poverty, he developed a compassionate love of neighbor evidenced by his numerous acts of social, charitable, and educational work. Yet he was most noted as a man of prayer, continuing in the tradition of the *staretz*. Unique was that John was a parish priest, not a monk, yet his counsel was sought by many from all societal classes across Russia. He was noted to be a major influence on lay Christians. His spirituality had three important features: (1) daily Eucharist is central, (2) charity is inherent to Christian piety, and (3) the importance of personal prayer. His spiritual diary, published as *My Life in Christ*, is a classic of contemporary Russian Orthodox spirituality

John Paul II, Pope St. (1920-2005) –born Karol Józef Wojtyla in Poland, he was previously the Cardinal Archbishop of Kraków. Elected to the papacy in 1978, he was the second longest-serving pope in modern history. As part of his special emphasis on the Universal Call to Holiness, he beatified and canonized over 1,800 people, more than in the preceding five centuries combined. As an extension of his successful work with youth as a young priest, he pioneered the International World Youth Day gatherings, beginning in Rome in 1985. Pope John Paul II wrote 14 encyclicals, of which a number are particularly germane to our discussions. In *Dives et Misericordia* (1980), he stressed divine mercy being the greatest feature of God, needed especially in modern times. In *Veritatis Splendor* (1993), he discussed the dependence of humanity on God ("Without the Creator, the creature disappears"). In *Ut Unum Sint* (1995) he explained that for the Church to achieve its deepest meaning, it needed to breathe again from both its lungs, one Eastern and one Western. In *Novo Millennio Ineunte* (2001), he discussed starting afresh with Christ and coined the term, "The New Evangelization."

Keating, Fr. Thomas, OCSO (1923-2018) – a Trappist monk and one of the founders of Contemplative Outreach, along with Trappist monks Basil Pennington (1931-2005) and William Meninger (1932—). Through his writings, Trappist monk Thomas Merton (1915-1968) created renewed interest in a contemplative prayer method traced back to *The Cloud of Unknowing*, an anonymous work of Christian mysticism written in Middle English in the latter half of the 14th century. Merton coined the term "Centering Prayer" for this technique. The founders of Contemplative Outreach helped bring Merton's prayer technique out of the monastery and made it accessible to others, especially laity.

Kelly, Matthew (1973—) – contemporary Catholic apologist, motivational speaker, author, and founder of Dynamic Catholic. He often discusses the value and positive inspiration of Catholicism on everyday life. He has written many books. Some of the most notable include *Rediscover Catholicism: A Spiritual Guide to Living with Passion* (2010), *The Four Signs of a Dynamic Catholic* (2013), *Rediscover Jesus* (2015), *Perfectly Yourself* (2017) and *Rediscover the Saints* (2019).

Lewis, C. S. (1898-1963) – a British novelist, poet, academic, medievalist, literary critic, essayist, lay theologian, broadcaster, lecturer, and Christian apologist. He held academic positions at both Oxford University and Cambridge University. Baptized in the Church of Ireland, he fell away as an adolescent. At age 32, he returned to Anglicanism and considered himself "an ordinary layman in the Church of England." Some of his best-known works are *The Screwtape Letters*, *The Chronicles of Narnia*, and *The Space Trilogy*. *Mere Christianity* was one of his Christian apologetic writings.

Moses, Monk, of Mount Athos (d. 2014) – born in Athens, he entered monastic life on Mount Athos in 1975. Much of his time was devoted to studying the lives of saints and poetry, to writing articles and books. He published many books and had over 300 newspaper articles about the spiritual life. Two of his collections of essays are available in English and published as *Athonite Flowers* (2000) and *Holiness: Is It Attainable Today?* (2012).

Nephon of Constantia, St. (unknown) – a son of a wealthy government official, St. Nephon was sent from Alexandria to Constantinople to further his studies. Having succumbed to the temptations of the great metropolis, he then pleased God with a life of deep repentance, ascetic struggles, watchfulness, and prayer. He was then ordained bishop of the Church of Constantia in Cyprus, where he distinguished himself as a shepherd of souls. His life was generally unknown as it was only recorded in ancient Byzantine manuscripts treasured in the monasteries of Mount Athos.

Paul VI, Pope St. (1897-1978) – born Giovanni Battista Enrico Antonio Maria Montini, he was a close advisor to both Pope Pius XII and Pope John XXIII. The former made him the Archbishop of Milan and the latter elevating him to the College of Cardinals. He was elected to the papacy in 1963 during the Second Vatican Council (1962-1965), after the death of Pope John XXIII, and was responsible for implementing many of the reforms that came from the council. He also fostered closer relationships with the Eastern Orthodox Churches. Notably, his meeting with Ecumenical Patriarch Athenagoras I of Constantinople in January 1964 in Jerusalem led to the rescinding of the excommunications of the Great Eastern Schism (1054). He strongly embraced the Universal Call to Holiness, which was included in *Lumen Gentium*, a document of the council and released in 1964. His 1975 apostolic exhortation on evangelization, *Evangelii Nuntiandi* (Evangelization in the Modern World), affirmed the role of every Christian, not just ordained ministers, in spreading the Gospel. It is considered the source of The New Evangelization;

however, the term itself was coined by Pope St. John Paul II.

Pope, Msgr. Charles (1961—) – a highly respected priest of the Archdiocese of Washington, DC who makes frequent appearances in Catholic media, and is a parish pastor. He has weekly contributions to the *National Catholic Register* and *Our Sunday Visitor*.

Porphyrios of Kavsokalyvia, Elder (1907-91) – an Athonite hieromonk (priest-monk) and spiritual elder known for his gifts of spiritual discernment. He is reflective of the hesychast tradition. The best-known work of his teachings is *Wounded by Love: The Life and Wisdom of Elder Porphyrios*.

Sakharov, Elder Sophrony of Essex (1896-1993) – Russian monk, theologian, and disciple of St. Silouan the Athonite. Born in Russian, he immigrated to Paris in 1922 and began studies at the St. Sergius Orthodox Theological Institute. Finding theological studies unfulfilling, he moved to the Monastery of St. Panteleimon at Mount Athos in 1926, becoming a disciple and later biographer of St. Silouan. He stayed at the monastery until 1938, when St. Silouan reposed, and then left the monastery grounds to reside in the Athonite desert; first at Karoulia, then at a cave near St Paul's Monastery. Ordained to the priesthood in 1941, he ultimately became a spiritual father to many Athonite monks. In 1947, he left Mount Athos and returned to Paris, where he published his work on St. Silouan. He also continued his studies under Vladimir Lossky. Later, he founded the Patriarchal Stavropegic Monastery of St. John the Baptist in Tolleshunt Knights, Malden, Essex under Metropolitan Anthony (Bloom) of Sourozh. He wrote several works including *We Shall See Him as He Is* (1985) and *On Prayer*, published posthumously.

Sarah, Cardinal Robert (1945—) – currently Prefect of the Congregation for Divine Worship and the Discipline of the Sacraments, part of the Roman Curia. Originally from Guinea, Africa, he was Archbishop of Conakry. Made a cardinal in 2010, he held several roles in the Vatican. He wrote three books in conversation with Nicolas Diat:

Choosing Life in Christ

God or Nothing: A Conversation on Faith (2015), *The Power of Silence: Against the Dictatorship of Noise* (2017), and *The Day is Now Far Spent* (2019).

Sheen, Archbishop Fulton J. (1895-1979) – an American archbishop well-known for his preaching, and work on radio and television. Some consider him one of the first televangelists. His teachings were visionary, forewarning in 1947 the end of the American political, economic, and social life based on Christian principles. He cited symptoms such as the break-up of the family, divorce, abortion, immorality, and overall general dishonesty. Sheen urged all to pray: "The forces of evil are united; the forces of good are divided. We may not be able to meet in the same pew—would to God we did—but we can meet on our knees."

Silouan the Athonite, St. (1866-1939) – a Russian-born monk who entered the Russian monastery of St. Panteleimon on Mount Athos. An ardent ascetic, he received the grace of unceasing prayer. After long years of spiritual trial, he acquired great humility and inner stillness. He prayed and wept for the world as for himself and put great value on love for enemies. He was barely literate, yet highly sought by pilgrims for his wise counsel and revered as a spiritual elder (*staretz*). His disciple was Archimandrite Sophrony, who edited his writings.

Teresa of Calcutta, St. (1910-97) – also known as Mother Teresa. A Roman Catholic sister and founder of the Missionaries of Charity. Mother Teresa was well known for her focus on the poorest of the poor, the unlovable, the unwanted, and the dying. She was recognized by the Secretary General of the United Nations as the most influential woman in the world and won the Nobel Peace Prize in 1979.

Theophan the Recluse, St. (1815-94) – a Russian monk, later Bishop of Tambov, during the Russian Spiritual Renaissance. Known for his spiritual counsel and books on the spiritual life. In his writings, he persistently focused on an interior life of continuous prayer and was rooted in the hesychast tradition. His best-known works include *The Pathway to Salvation: A Manual of Spiritual Transformation* and editing Nicodemus the Hagiorite's work, *Unseen Warfare*, inserting many Patristic references. His sayings are a significant portion of the content in the Orthodox anthology: *The Art of Prayer*, compiled by Igumen Chariton. Theophan also translated the *Philokalia* from Church Slavonic into Russian.

Glossary of Selected Terms

The following are selected terms related to our conferences:

Agapé (ἀγάπη)   Greek term for the highest form of love. See "love."

Almsgiving   A penitential practice, sacrificially giving to God through charitable acts, assisting others in need. It is more than giving money or philanthropy. Rather, it is a conversion of heart, moved to compassion as Jesus was, and giving from our means, not just our surplus (see the widow's contribution, Luke 21:1-4). Almsgiving also becomes part of our prayer practice. Love of neighbor is an outflow from our love of God.

Art of Spiritual Life   Establishing a rhythm in daily living that includes key spiritual practices such as prayer, fasting, and almsgiving. See also "Interior Monasticism." Includes regular study of the ascetical practices of the Fathers of the Church. The objectives are increasing awareness of our interior longing for God, ability to recognize his presence in our daily activities, and a focus on surrender of self-will to God's will. Through these efforts, we increasingly collaborate with God's plan for our lives (see *synergeia*) in order to draw closer to him, to experience joy and fulfillment, and prepare ourselves for our destiny: union with God in the life to come.

Asceticism   From the Greek *áskēsis* (ἄσκησις), meaning "exercise" or "training," similar to that done by an athlete. Asceticism as practice of spiritual discipline has three basic goals: (1) bringing order and self-control to human passions/appetites, (2) centering a person, and (3) opening a person to God's presence. Ascetical disciplines were meant as voluntary self-denial as prescribed by Jesus in his terms and conditions of discipleship ("If anyone wishes to come after me, he must *deny* himself and take up his cross daily and follow me" – Luke 9:23).

Body of Christ

An analogy of all believers united together in a single body with Christ Jesus as its head. A body has many members, but remains a single body (unity which retains diversity). Christ speaks of the unity all believers in his analogy of the vine and branches (John 15:1-10). Images of the Church as the body of Christ come from Rom. 12:5, 1 Cor. 12-27, Col. 1:18, 1:24, and Eph. 5:23. As such, the Church is one with Christ.

Charity

In the context of a theological virtue, we love God more than everything, and our neighbor for the love of God. See also *"Agapé."* Charity is one of the three theological virtues, along with faith and hope. Per St. Paul, charity (love) is the greatest of these virtues. See 1 Cor. 13:1-13.

Complacency

A feeling of uncritical satisfaction with oneself or one's achievements. In the spiritual journey, there is a danger of presuming one has made sufficient progress towards salvation wherein further effort is not required. Jesus warns against this in the Parable of the Rich Fool (Luke 12:16-21). Synonyms for complacency include self-satisfaction, self-approval, self-approbation, self-admiration, and self-congratulation. When a primary objective of the spiritual journey is surrender of self-will to the Divine will, just by its definition, one can see the dangers of complacency, wherein the focus is on "self."

Contemplation

Refers to various practices that aim at "looking at," "gazing at," or "being aware of" God or the divine presence. Contemplative prayer follows meditation and is the highest form of prayer that aims to achieve a close spiritual union with God.

Conversion

Transformation or change of heart, *metanoia* (μετάνοια). For most, conversion is an ongoing, life-long process and not a "big bang" one-time event. We must continually choose to follow Jesus on a daily basis. ("If anyone wishes to come after me, he must deny himself and take up his cross *daily* and follow me" – Luke 9:23).

Deification

See "Divinization." These terms are used interchangeably.

Deposit of Faith (*Depositum Fidei*)

The content of divine revelation (revealed truth) coming to us from the Sacred Scriptures and Sacred Tradition. Combined, these are a single deposit of faith that form the basis of our Catholic beliefs. It is considered sacred because it comes from God, and a deposit because it has been left to us by Christ.

Desert Spirituality

Spirituality drawing predominantly from the lives of the Desert Fathers and Mothers from the Early Church. This includes the hesychast prayer tradition (Jesus Prayer) and spiritual disciplines such as ascetical practices, detachment, mourning our sinfulness, and a spirit of penance. Throughout the history of Eastern Christian Spirituality, the Ancient Church to modern times, one can observe that it is deeply rooted in desert spirituality. That is one reason we call this a "back-to-basics" spirituality—simple yet continuously relevant to the spiritual journey and personal vocation to holiness.

Desire   See "Longing."

Despair   A complete loss or absence of hope. The Good News of the Gospel is intended to give us hope, that a life of eternal blessedness awaits us. However, the demons try to exploit our weaknesses in order to diminish our hope, leading us into despair.

Despondency   This is a state where one's spirits are low, reflecting a loss of hope or courage. It is one the weaknesses the demons try to exploit in order to disrupt our relationship with God. As St. Seraphim of Sarov wrote: "Despondency is a worm gnawing the heart."[355]

Detachment   From the Greek *apatheia* (ἀπάθεια), a state of mind free from passions, such as a movement of the soul toward irrational love or senseless hate. In order to grow in the spiritual life, especially in contemplative prayer, a person must strive for personal purification in order to be freed from the passions and attain the virtues. *Apatheia* is a state of total dependence on God's grace—impossible to obtain on our own. It is only possible to attain through *synergeia*.

***Diakonia* (διακονία)** The Greek term means "service." In theological terms, it is a call to serve the poor and oppressed. The call of the first "deacons" in Acts 6:6, was to take care of the Greek widows,

---

355 Valentine Zander, *St. Seraphim of Sarov*, transl. Sr. Gabriel Anne, SSC (Crestwood, NY: St. Vladimir's Seminary Press, 1975), 103.

who were neglected in the daily distribution of bread. So, first and foremost, this concept is about serving the poor and marginalized. It is the type of heart and mindset to which all followers of Jesus should aspire. See also "Almsgiving."

Distractions
From the Greek *logismoi* (λογίσμοι), invading or intrusive thoughts that disturb or sidetrack one in prayer. One must always be vigilant (*nepsis*) in order to maintain inner stillness (*hesychia*).

Divine Image
Humanity is created in the divine image (see "Image of God"). "God created mankind in his image; in the image of God he created them; male and female he created them" (Gen. 1:27). Early Church Fathers would say that we are patterned after the Image Absolute, which is Jesus Christ.

Divinization
Related to the concept of *theosis*, the process of practicing the God-like virtues, becoming more "God-like," in order to prepare ourselves for our destiny: union with God.

Elder
A Spiritual Father. See "*Staretz*."

Encounter
To come upon or meet with. In the context of these conferences, the premise is that God is meant to be experienced in a tangible way. "The Joy of the Gospel fills the hearts and lives of all who encounter Jesus" (Pope Francis, *Evangelii Gaudium*, no. 1). Thus, this theme of encounter is central to these conferences and other related works.

Enlightenment (Divine Illumination)

The divine assistance or grace that we are provided to discern whether our thoughts and actions are aligned with the Divine will, and to gain greater insights with respect to the divine mysteries generally based on contemplation or encounters with the Divine Presence. Sometimes referred to as Holy Illumination. Not to be confused with the philosophical movement known as The Enlightenment (see below).

Enlightenment (Philosophical)

The Enlightenment was an intellectual and philosophical movement that dominated the ideas of Europe in the eighteenth century. It fostered a belief in the inherent goodness of humanity and confidence that human beings had the capacity for greatness within themselves, dismissing the role of God (reason over faith). Over time, this spawned several other movements or philosophical schools of thought including Humanism, Rationalism, and Individualism. Humanism: an outlook or system of thought attaching prime importance to human rather than divine or supernatural matters. Rationalism a belief or theory that opinions and actions should be based on reason and knowledge rather than on religious belief or emotional response. Individualism: (1) the habit or principle of being independent and self-reliant and (2) a social theory favoring freedom of action for individuals over collective or state control. All of these schools of thought, which have influenced our culture today, illustrate a movement away from God and even communal responsibilities, with an increased focus on self. Accordingly, within our secular society we have developed a culture of individualism, which subconsciously influences our perspectives and actions.

Eternal Blessedness To live in union with God (eternal blessedness), which is our human purpose or destiny. Sometimes this is also referred to as "communion with God," whereby we share in the very life of the Holy Trinity. *Theosis* is the incremental process of striving to prepare ourselves for union with God.

Faith Confidence or trust in a person or thing. For these conferences, faith means confidence and trust in God. Faith is one of the three theological virtues, along with hope and charity (love) — gifts from God that lead us to him and allow us to live in closer relationship with him.

Fasting Ascetical/penitential practice of abstaining from food, creating a physical hunger and being reminded of the spiritual void only Christ can fill. If we fast with our heart, we express our love for God and acknowledge our sinfulness. Our sacrifice unites us to the sacrifice of Jesus Christ, who shed his blood for our salvation. Further, self-denial disposes us to freedom from worldly distractions to create an environment conducive to prayer. Finally, through voluntary fasting, we unite ourselves in solidarity with the poor and suffering who have no food, being reminded that we are all members of the body of Christ, and are reliant upon God for all our blessings.

Fear of the Lord A reverential fear or awe of God in his majesty. It is not a phobia or a negative fear. It implies a rightly ordered relationship between God (Creator) and the person (created). Fear of the Lord is considered one of the seven gifts of the Holy Spirit. Fear of God is used interchangeably herein. As St. Isaac the Syrian wrote, "The fear of God is the beginning of virtue."

Forgiveness   From the Greek *aphesis* (ἄφεσις), meaning "dismissal" or "release" or figuratively "pardon." This is the concept of forgiveness, freeing the mind from anger and resentment, demons that can impair our interior stillness. Jesus tells the Parable of the Unforgiving Servant (Matt. 18:21-35) and concludes by saying, "So will my Heavenly Father do to you, unless each of you forgives his brother from his heart" (Matt. 18:35). Note the emphasis on *heart*, which means genuine forgiveness versus superficial and is intended to assist one in remaining "clean of heart," an important concept in *theosis*.

Formation   The process of forming or the state of being formed. In the context used herein, formation is the spiritual grounding of an individual (experiential based on encounter) as opposed to catechesis, which is formal instruction, based on an academic approach to theology (intellectual knowledge). Thus, formation is coming to know and entering into a relationship with Jesus Christ, learning to live our lives with him as our guide (learning to become more Christ-like) versus solely an intellectual understanding of doctrines of faith. As Isaac the Syrian would say, "You cannot taste honey by reading a book." See also *"Praxis."*

Freedom   The state of being free or at liberty without confinement or under physical restraint; exemption from external control, interference, regulation, etc.; the power to determine action without restraint. Surrender of self-will to the Divine will is an act of freedom.

Hesychia (ἡσυχία)   Stillness, watchfulness, interior silence of the heart. Hesychast prayer, also known more commonly as the Jesus Prayer, is a contemplative prayer practice. Hesychasm evolved from the practices of the Desert Fathers and Mothers (during the third to seventh centuries) and was further developed in the monasteries on Mount Athos during the Greek Spiritual Renaissance (1200-1400). It advanced further in Russia during the Russian Spiritual Renaissance (1700-1917) and is still faithfully preserved and practiced within the Eastern Christian Churches, both Catholic and Orthodox. Also called "Prayer of the Heart."

Holiness   The state in which we strive to fulfill our destiny, which is union with God. It is an ongoing journey of transformation involving spiritual struggle and increasing devotion to God. See also "Universal Call to Holiness."

Holy Mysteries   Term used by the Eastern Churches for Sacraments. Comes from the Greek *mystērion* (μυστήριον), meaning "mystery." Emphasis is placed on the mystery of the ritual. The "holy mysteries" are considered vessels for mystical participation in divine grace.

Hope   The combination of a desire for something and an expectation of receiving it. St. Paul writes that hope is for that which is unseen (Rom. 8:24) and, in the context of these conferences, the ultimate hope is in our supernatural destiny of union with God. It is hope that brings us to desire eternal life as our ultimate happiness. "And hope does not disappoint," as St. Paul wrote (Rom. 5:5). Hope is one of the three theological virtues along with faith and charity (love).

Human Heart	A commonly held belief, beginning with the Early Desert Fathers and Mothers, is that Christianity was a divinizing process taking place gradually within the human heart, the interior focus where man and the Triune God meet.
Humility	From the earth; grounded. A simple, low opinion of one's self, avoiding honors, ranks, titles. It is the foundation for the other virtues.
Image of God	The sum total of our possibilities. It is imprinted upon us and can never be taken away. As humans, we have a capacity for God (*capex Dei*) and the ability to enter into relationship with him because we are related to him. In this context, we describe ourselves as being created in the divine image.
Incarnation	The doctrine that the second person of the Trinity, the *Logos*, assumed human form in the person of Jesus Christ and is completely God and completely man without mixture or confusion. Renowned 20th century Catholic Theologian Karl Rahner, SJ, uses the term: "divinized humanity," essentially describing our goal as humans—divinization (i.e., *theosis*).
Indwelling Divine Presence	The presence of the Divine within the human heart. Through Baptism, we have the Indwelling Presence. We cultivate this presence by following the example of Jesus, through self-surrender, and aligning our will with the Divine will.

Interior Monasticism For one who is not a monastic, adopting an interior life based on prayer and spiritual disciplines such as penance, ascetical practices, and detachment, all designed to deepen one's relationship with God. See also, "Art of Spiritual Life."

Interior Stillness See "*Hesychia.*"

Jesus Prayer Lord Jesus Christ, Son of God, have mercy on me, a sinner. See "*Hesychia.*"

Kenosis (κένωσις) Renunciation of the divine nature, at least in part, by Christ in the Incarnation: "Who, though he was in the form of God, did not deem equality with God something to be grasped. Rather, he emptied himself, taking the form of a slave" (Phil. 2:6-7). This should be considered in light of the Fall of Adam, who wanted to be "like God" (the temptation). Thus, Jesus models for us the right relationship with God (dependent on God through self-emptying), and we are called to do likewise.

Likeness of God Image of God's fulfillment, our ability to become who God wants us to be, achieving our possibilities, bringing us to our purpose: eternal blessedness. As discussed above, means to live ultimately in union with him— nothing less. We may choose not to seek to achieve our possibilities, but the Image of God can never be taken from us.

Listlessness Reflective of a lack of energy, drive, or purpose. In the absence of hope, many find themselves drifting through life without a sense of purpose or meaning. The Good News of the Gospel is that humanity does have a purpose; we are created in the image of God to share eternal blessedness with him. God alone can fulfill our deepest longing.

Liturgy "Work of the people," from the Greek *liturgeia* (λιτυργεια). Eastern Christian Eucharistic worship is generally called the Divine Liturgy, reflecting how heaven and earth come together in worship.

Logismoi (λογίσμοι) See "Distractions."

Longing A desire in every human heart that aspires to something more. Every person has a desire for happiness and fulfillment, to love and be loved. Longing is a spiritual void created by God in humans so that he alone can fill it with his love. Anything else by which we try to fill that longing just creates temporary fulfillment that, once the feeling of fulfillment has passed, often results in dissatisfaction and frustration. That is because we attempt to fill infinite longing with finite things. As part of the spiritual journey, we come to an increased realization that our longing is truly for the Divine Presence and that we can only be who we were created to be through him. He alone can fill our deepest longing, our human yearning for more.

Love (*Agapé*) The highest form of love, charity; the love of God for man and of man for God. This is contrasted to *eros* (ἔρως) or romantic love, *philía* (φιλία), which is love as a bond of friendship, and *storgē* (στοργή), which is love as a bond of empathy.

Metanoia (μετάνοια) True change of heart; conversion. Change in one's way of life resulting from penitence or spiritual conversion. Consider the example of Zacchaeus. (See Luke 19:1–10). See also "Conversion."

Mourning our Sinfulness	See *"Penthos."*
Mount Athos	The epicenter of Eastern Orthodox monastic spirituality. Mount Athos is a mountain and peninsula in Greece, the location of 20 significant monasteries under the direct jurisdiction of the Ecumenical Patriarch of Constantinople. The term "Athonite" refers to Mount Athos.
Mystic	One who has had an experience of the Divine. Throughout these conferences, we have discussed having an awareness of the presence of God. The adjective is "mystical." As Rahner wrote, "The devout Christian of the future will either be a 'mystic,' one who has 'experienced' something, or he [she] will cease to be anything at all."
Mysticism	Becoming one with God; mystical union or direct communion with God. This occurs when one achieves the highest level of prayer, known as pure prayer or unitive prayer. Not all will achieve this height of prayer, because it is a gift granted by God commensurate with one's efforts.
***Nepsis* (Νιψις)**	Sober vigilance and spiritual attentiveness. As a person draws closer to God, it is important to remain vigilant for assaults from the Evil One, which often can be subtle and try to intervene in our relationship with God.

New Evangelization   This term was first used by Pope John Paul II in his Apostolic Letter, *Novo Millennio Ineunte* (Jan. 6, 2001). It is an invitation for all Catholics to renew their relationship with Jesus Christ and his Church. It is a call to each person to deepen his or her faith, have confidence in the Gospel, and possess a willingness to share the Gospel. It begins with a personal encounter with the person of Jesus. In turn, renewed by our encounter, we are particularly called to reach out to the baptized who have fallen away from Church. Pope Benedict XVI clarified that the New Evangelization is new, not in its content, but new in its inner thrust and methods to correspond to the times, specifically, confronting the cultural crisis created by secularization. He also established a Pontifical Council for Promoting the New Evangelization in 2010.

Patristics   Reference to Early Church Fathers, both Latin and Greek, and their writings. The Patristic Period began at the end of the Apostolic Period (time of the Apostles, ca. 100). For the Western Church, the Patristic Period ends after the Second Council of Nicaea (787), the last of the First Seven Ecumenical Councils of the undivided Church. This period is considered significant because consensus was reached through these councils on the primary doctrines of the Church. Through a movement leading up to the Second Vatican Council, the concept of *ressourcement*, a return to the sources, generally means a return to the teachings of Sacred Scripture and the Church Fathers. As an interesting aside, the Eastern Church considers this Patristic Period to have extended into the fifteenth century through Simeon of Thessalonica, as evidenced by the writers included in Migne's *Patrologia Graeca*.

Personal Holiness   See "Universal Call to Holiness."

Prayer   Spending time with God, entering more deeply into relationship with him. While there are many forms of prayer, our primary focus herein has been on contemplation and *hesychia* (hesychast prayer/Jesus Prayer). Other types of prayer include liturgical prayer and recitation of the Divine Office. Prayer is considered a penitential practice in terms of returning to God, rending our hearts, and acknowledging our sinfulness. Through prayer, we begin to establish a right-ordered relationship between us and our Creator.

Praxis   The process by which a theory, lesson, or skill is enacted, practiced, embodied, or realized. This is true in the spiritual life as we live our lives in conformity with Christ, adopting his teachings and the lessons he modeled for us, and reinforced through prayer. Like any skill that we desire to perfect, we must continually practice and remain steadfast in our efforts. Thus, our vocation to holiness is brought to life.

Penthos (πένθος)   Also called compunction, this is mourning for our sinfulness ("Spare your people, O Lord") and an important part of repentance as a state of mind. Some Greek Fathers also describe the gift of tears associated with such mourning, a reflection of unworthiness, and a desire for the mercy of God. This also helps to cultivate the virtue of humility.

Pure Prayer   This is the highest level of participation according to the hesychast prayer tradition. It is an experience of union with God in peace, love, and joy occurring in this present life. This level of participation is a gift from God and is not given to all. Those who have achieved this level of participation describe intense feelings and an experience of light.

Purification

To purify, refine, and be set free from any impurities that could contaminate our lives. Consider how gold is refined by fire, increasingly removing impurities, and becoming more valuable. The same is true in pursuing our vocation to holiness. This is indicative of our incremental journey of transformation, preparing ourselves for eternal blessedness (union with God, sharing in the life of the Holy Trinity). See also "Conversion," "Deification," "Divinization," "*Metanoia*," "Sanctification," "*Theosis*," and "Transformation."

Ressourcement

French for a "return to the sources." This was a movement by French and German theologians that included a renewed interest in biblical exegesis, mysticism, and Patristics. One could say that this was a return to the basics. This movement is also called *Nouvelle Théologie* (New Theology), a counterpoint to the dominant dogmatic theology that existed prior to the Second Vatican Council (Scholasticism). This focus on a return to the sources had a significant influence on the Council. See Patristics."

Rule of Prayer

The outline of our daily prayer routine—a structured rule that is practiced each day. It should specify a time, generally morning and evening, and, if possible, a place for prayer. As with any skill, prayer is something that should be practiced regularly.

Sacraments

Term used by the Western Church from the Latin, *sacramentum*, meaning "sign of the sacred." The Sacraments are considered to have a visible and invisible reality—a reality open to the human senses (visible) but grasped in its God-given depths with the eyes of faith (invisible).

Sanctification

By definition, to make holy, to purify, or to free from sin. In pursuing a vocation to holiness, we are sanctifying our lives in order to prepare ourselves for eternal blessedness. It is a deliberate choice, saying "yes" to Christ, and an ongoing process of purification. See also *"Theosis."*

Self-surrender

Same as self-denial. We freely choose to surrender our own will (self-will) to the Divine will. Jesus says to be his disciple, one must deny himself, take up his cross daily, and follow him (Cf. Luke 9:23). See also *Kenosis.*

Sober Vigilance

See *"Nepsis."*

Sobornost

A term that evolved during the Russian Spiritual Renaissance beginning in the 1800s, it emphasizes the cooperation of people over individualism. The image used to illustrate this concept is the parish church in the middle of the village, drawing all people together and helping to provide for the needs of all, first and foremost being the spiritual needs.

Spiritual Accompaniment

Joining together as a community of pilgrims on our journey to draw closer to God. As Pope Francis wrote, we support one another, "removing our sandals before others in humility," walking with each other "in a steady and reassuring manner, reflecting our closeness and a compassionate gaze which heals, liberates, and encourages our growth in the Christian life" (*Evangelii Gaudium*, no. 169). Spiritual accompaniment is important because as pilgrims on journey, we are no longer orphaned, helpless, and homeless. We are not drifters, because communally we have a sense of direction with the desire to draw closer to God.

Spiritual Direction The practice of accompanying people as they attempt to deepen their relationship with the Divine, or to learn and grow in their own personal spirituality. The spiritual companion (or spiritual director) accompanies the directee and is generally a Spiritual Father or Mother, often a priest, monk, or nun. See also "Elder" and "*Staretz.*"

Spiritual Warfare See "Unseen Warfare."

Stillness See "*Hesychia.*"

Starchestvo A lineage of spiritual wisdom of prayer maintained by an elder (*staretz*). The Greek and Russian monastic traditions have a long unbroken history of elders and disciples, often centered on certain monasteries (Athonite, Optina, Sarov, Pechersk Lavra, etc.). This was often how the hesychast tradition was transmitted from one generation to the next.

Staretz A spiritual elder from whom people seek spiritual guidance. For example, beginning in the Russian Spiritual Renaissance, lay-people would come to the monastery for spiritual counsel. An elder may also have disciples who place themselves in obedience to him. This is the foundation for *starchestvo*.

Synergeia (συνεργεια) — Greek for "synergy." In the context of our discussions, this is the relationship between the grace of God and human freedom; the person's collaboration with the Divine to achieve his or her final destiny. God does not force his grace upon us, but guides and strengthens us when we submit to his will (self-surrender). It is about divine initiative and the human response to that initiative (acceptance of the gift). People cannot achieve salvation without divine assistance. Jesus tells us, "Without me, you can do nothing" (John 15:5). Pelagianism (named after the British monk Pelagius, 354-420) was a heresy in the Church that taught humanity could choose the good and achieve salvation through their individual efforts and without divine assistance. Pope Francis warns against modern Pelagianism in his apostolic exhortation, *Gaudete et Exsultate* (March 19, 2018).

Theological Virtues — See "Virtues."

Theosis (Θέωσις) — Divinization or deification. The ongoing process of transformation or conversion wherein we increasingly practice the God-like virtues in order to prepare for our destiny: union with God. See 2 Pet. 1:4, "[Jesus] has bestowed on us the precious and very great promises, so that through them you may come to share in the divine nature ..." *Theosis* is a process that begins in our temporal life and culminates in the life to come at the Resurrection of the Dead. Essentially, *theosis* is the core of the Good News of the Gospel, namely that we are called to share in the very life of God. It is the affirmative response to God, who communicates himself to us. Divinization and deification are used interchangeably.

Theotokos (Θεοτόκος)	Greek term meaning "God-bearer." Title of the Blessed Virgin Mary given to her at the Council of Ephesus (431). From this, we derive the term "Mother of God." It is important to note that at the Council, Mary was declared the *Theotokos* (God-bearer), not *Christotokos* (Christ-bearer). The reason was to reinforce the proper understanding of the Incarnation of Jesus Christ, who was both fully human and fully divine. The term *Theotokos* is often used in Eastern Christian prayers (e.g., "through the prayers of the *Theotokos*, O Savior save us").
Transformation	The ongoing process of conversion in order to achieve our destiny: union with God. See *"Theosis," "Metanoia,"* and *"Conversion."*
Union with God	See "Eternal Blessedness."
Universal Call to Holiness	The belief that all people, regardless of vocation or status, are called to personal holiness, for we all have the same destiny: union with God. It is based on Jesus's teaching, "So be perfect, just as your Heavenly Father is perfect" (Matt. 5:48). This particular term was described in the Second Vatican Council's document, "Dogmatic Constitution on the Church" (*Lumen Gentium*), Chapter V, November 21, 1964. "All the faithful of Christ of whatever rank or status, are called to the fullness of the Christian life and to the perfection of charity ..." (no. 40). However, this concept is not new. We see evidence of this call already playing out in everyday life throughout the history of the Church. For example, already 200 years before the Second Vatican Council in Russia, lay-people, from peasants to nobility, came to the monasteries such as Optina or Sarov, seeking spiritual counsel from the monks. The work *The Pilgrim's Tale* is a story about an unknown peasant who seeks to understand the mysteries of the Jesus Prayer. Of noteworthiness, in all the examples of this call to holiness, those following the spiritual journey seek guidance and wisdom from those more experienced such as the monks, the nuns, and even parish priests such as St. John of Kronstadt.

Unseen Warfare	The interior struggles a person has with temptations and passions, as referenced by the Church Fathers and Mothers. Sometimes also called spiritual warfare. Divinization is an ongoing struggle, striving to move from self-centered, self-will to self-surrender to the Divine will. Sometimes the battle can be fierce, like the clash of tectonic plates (self-will and divine-will). Sometimes it can be more subtle, as weeds slowly creeping into a well-managed lawn (see Parable of the Weeds among the Wheat, Matt. 13:24-30) — a reminder of the importance of constant vigilance. The Spiritual Fathers and Mothers advise us that this is a lifelong struggle; the demons will exploit any opportunity or weakness to interfere in our relationship with God.

Vigilance	Constant watchfulness against attacks from the Evil One. See "*Nepsis*."

Virtues	Gifts from God that lead us to live in closer relationship with him. The three theological virtues (faith, hope, and charity) come from God and lead us to God. These virtues are discussed in 1 Cor. 13:1-13.

Vocation to Holiness	The universal call and invitation by God to eternal blessedness (salvation). People are called to this life and invited by Jesus to follow him, preparing ourselves through a lifetime of conversion, struggles (see "Unseen Warfare"), and transformation for our ultimate destiny: eternal blessedness (union with God). See also: "Universal Call to Holiness."

Watchfulness	Term used by some spiritual writers for sober vigilance. See "*Nepsis*" and "*hesychia*."

Historical Perspective

Selected Christian Spiritual Traditions: East and West

The following is a list of certain significant spiritual traditions within the Church including the names of selected key individuals and writings from the respective periods.

	East	West
Monastic Origins of Spirituality		
200 – 800s	**Desert Spirituality** • St. Antony of Egypt (251-356) • St. Macarius the Great (c.300-391) • Various monastic leaders from the Egyptian desert (330s-460s), *Sayings of the Desert Fathers (Apophthegmata Patrum)* • The two Old Men: St. Barsanuphius the Great and St. John of Gaza (mid-6th century), *Letters* • St. Dorotheos of Gaza (d. 565), *Discourses and Sayings* • St. John Climacus (579-606), *The Ladder of Divine Ascent* (ca. 600) • St. Isaac the Syrian (640-700), *Ascetical Homilies* • After the Islamic conquest of Egypt in seventh century, some monks moved from the Egyptian desert to Mount Athos	**Desert Spirituality Moves West** • St. Augustine of Hippo (354-430), *Confessions* • St. John Cassian (360-435), *Conferences* and *Institutes* • St. Benedict of Nursia (480-543), founder of the Benedictine Order (Rule of St. Benedict), beginnings of *Lectio Divina*.

	East	West
900 – 1200	**Eastern Monastic Spirituality** • First monasteries established on Mount Athos, which ultimately becomes the center of Eastern Orthodox spirituality • St. Symeon the New Theologian (949-1022), monk of the Monastery of St. Mammas, Constantinople, *Discourses* • St. Anthony of Kiev (983-1073), founded Pechersk Lavra, the Monastery of the Caves (Kiev), bringing Athonite spirituality to Russia	**Western Monastic Spirituality** • St. Bruno (1030-1101), founds Carthusian order • Robert of Molesme (1028-1111), a Benedictine abbot, founds the Cistercian order (1098) • St. Bernard of Clairvaux (1090-1153), reforms the Cistercian order
Spirituality in the Scholastic Period		
1200 – 1400	**Greek Renaissance – Jesus Prayer** • Mount Athos becomes epicenter of hesychast spirituality • St. Gregory of Sinai (c.1265-1346) • St. Gregory Palamas (1296-1359), *Triads* • Hesychast Controversy (1330-54) • St. Nicholas Cabasilas (1322-92), *The Life in Christ* and *Commentary on the Divine Liturgy* **Russia** • St. Sergius of Radonezh (1314-92), a hermit and mystic, founds Holy Trinity Monastery near Moscow **Serbia and Romania** • Nicodemus of Tismana (c.1320-1406), a disciple of Athonite St. Gregory of Sinai, founds one monastery in Serbia and two in Romania in the hesychast tradition	**Age of Scholasticism** *Separation of Spirituality and Theology* • St. Dominic (1170-1221), founder of the Dominican Order • St. Francis of Assisi (1182-1226), founder of the Franciscan Order • John Van Ruysbroeck (1293-1381), Flemish Mysticism • St. Catherine of Sienna (1347-80) • Julian of Norwich (1342-1416), *Showings* • Anonymous *Cloud of Unknowing* (late 14th century, Carthusian); first reference to practice which later became known as Centering Prayer • Thomas à Kempis (1380-1471), *Imitation of Christ*

	East	West
Spirituality in the Age of Reformation		
1400 – 1800	**Hesychia in Russia** • St. Nil Sorsky (1433-1503), disciple of St. Sergius and represents school of spirituality focused on the hesychast spiritual movement (Jesus Prayer, study of scripture and patristics, silence, and living simply). Contemplative mystics. *Predanie* (The Tradition) and *Ustav* (The Monastic Rule). Considered a teacher of prayer. • St. Joseph Volotsky (1440-1515), another disciple of St. Sergius and represents a different school of spirituality focused on strict obligation of obedience to God, and meticulous observance of rituals and liturgical worship. Large monasteries with estates. • Rivalry emerged between the two schools with Volotsky's dominating and carrying favor with the Muscovite state. Hesychast spirituality disappears from public view in Russia for almost 200 years, until the Russian Spiritual Renaissance.	**Age of Reformation** **Ignatian Spirituality** • St. Ignatius of Loyola (1491-1556), founder of the Jesuits, *Spiritual Exercises* **Carmelite Spirituality in Spain** • St. Teresa of Ávila (1515-82), *Interior Castle* • St. John of the Cross (1542-91), *Dark Night of the Soul* and *Ascent of Mount Carmel* **Other Threads** • St. Philip Neri (1515-95), founder of the Congregation of the Oratory • Lorenzo Scupoli (1530-1610), *Spiritual Combat* • St. Francis de Sales (1567-1622), founder of the Salesians, *Introduction to the Devout Life* • Pierre de Bérulle (1575-1629), founder of the French Oratory • St. Vincent de Paul (1580-1660) and St. Louise de Marillac (1591-1660) • Armand Jean le Bouthillier de Rancé (1626-1700), concerned about laxity, reforms the Cistercians in 1664 and creates the Order of Cistercians of the Strict Observance (OCSO), also known as the Trappists • St. Paul of the Cross (1694-1775), founder of the Passionists in 1720 • St. Alphonsus Liguori (1696-1787), founder of the Redemptorists, *The Way of the Cross*

	East	West
Spirituality in the Age of Reason		

1700 – 1917	**Russian Spiritual Renaissance**
	Athonite Developments
	• St. Nicodemos the Hagiorite (1749-1809), *Philokalia* (1782), *Unseen Warfare* (1796), and *The Handbook of Spiritual Counsel* (1801)
	• Kollyvades Movement – spiritual renewal emphasizing Patristic theology, liturgical life, and frequent reception of communion; reaction against the European Enlightenment
	Russia
	• Paisius Velichkovsky (1722-94) translates *Philokalia* into Russian
	  – Optina Monastery (~1750s), becomes a significant spirituality center through disciples of Paisius
	  – Optina Elders, renowned spiritual masters (*Staretz*)
	• Appearance of the *Starchestvo*, spiritual threads based on an elder (*Staretz*)
	• St. Seraphim of Sarov (1759-1833)
	  – Sarov becomes a significant spirituality center
	• Laity embrace Jesus Prayer and monastic spiritual practices
	• Anonymous classic *The Pilgrim's Tale* (~1860s); earliest redaction from Optina Monastery
	• St. Ignatius Brianchaninov (1807-67), *The Field* and *The Arena*.
	• St. Theophan the Recluse (1815-94), *Unseen Warfare* (updated)
	• St. John of Kronstadt (1829-1908), *My Life in Christ*
		Age of Reason
		
		• Jean-Baptiste Henri Lacordaire (1802-61), re-establishes the Dominican order in Post-Revolutionary France
		• Isaac Hecker (1819-88), co-founder of the Paulists, focuses on the evangelization of America
		Oxford Movement
		• Included a focus on writings of the Early Church (patristics) and mystical writers; recovery of an integrated spirituality (body, mind, and heart), interior transformation, and emphasis on the potential of union with God
		• Pre-cursor to *ressourcement*, leading into the Second Vatican Council
		• St. John Henry Newman (1801-90), key figure in the Oxford Movement; also a founder of two Oratories in the United Kingdom, Birmingham (1848) and London (1849)
		Carmelite Spirituality in France
		• St. Thérèse of Lisieux, OCD (1873-97), *Story of a Soul*
		• St. Elizabeth of the Trinity, OCD (1880-1906)

	East	West
	Spirituality in the Modern Age	
1917 – Today	**Flourishing of Hesychast Tradition** **Russia and Eastern Europe** • Post-Communism (~1990s), prolific growth in monasteries in Russia, Ukraine, Romania, and Bulgaria **Russia** • Valaam Monastery returned to Orthodox Church (1989), the "Athos of the North" **Bulgaria** • Elder Seraphim Aleksiev (1912-93), *The Meaning of Suffering, Strife and Reconciliation*, and *The Forgotten Medicine: The Mystery of Repentance* **Romania** • Burning Bush movement at Antim Monastery (1945-58), a gathering of spiritual fathers focused on the revival of the hesychast tradition • Elder Cleopa Ilie (1912-98) • Elder Arsenie Papacioc (1914-2011) **Serbia (influenced by Optina/Valaam)** • Elder Thaddeus of Vitovnica (1914-2003)	**Age of Modernity** *Nouvelle Théologie* **(1935-60)** • "New Theology," a movement of critical reaction to Neo-Scholasticism with a desire to return Catholic theology to the original sources (Sacred Scripture and Church Fathers), most notably within circles of French and German theologians • Renewed interest in biblical exegesis and mysticism • Pre-cursor to *ressourcement* and its influence on reforms at the Second Vatican Council. **Second Vatican Council (1962-65)** • *Lumen Gentium* includes "Universal Call to Holiness" (Nov. 21, 1964) **Trappist/Contemplative Outreach (Cistercian Spirituality)** • Thomas Merton, OCSO (1915-68), coined the term "Centering Prayer" • Thomas Keating, OCSO (1923-2018) • Basil Pennington, OCSO (1931-2005) • William Meninger, OCSO (1932-) **World Community for Christian Meditation ("WCCM")** • Fr. John Main, OSB (1926-82) • Fr. Laurence Freeman, OSB (1951-)

	East	West
1917 – Today	**Athonite Revival of *Hesychia*** • St. Silouan the Athonite (1866-1938) – Elder Sophrony of Essex (1896-1993), *We Shall See Him As He Is* • Elder Joseph the Hesychast (1897-1959) • Elder Porphyrios of Kavsokalyvia (1906-91), *Wounded by Love* • Elder Paisios of Mount Athos (1924-94) • Elder Ephraim of Katounakia (1912-98) • Beginning in 2000, resurgence of monasteries on Mount Athos (Greece) **Egyptian Monastic Revival** • Monastic revival beginning in 1969 • Fr. Matthew the Poor (Fr. Matta El Meskeen) (1919-2006), *Orthodox Prayer Life* • Fr. Lazarus al Anthony, video interviews (e.g., *The Last Anchorite* and Coptic Youth Channel's series, *A Monk's Life*)	**Other Contemplatives** • Charles de Foucauld (1858-1916), hermit in North Africa • Caryll Houselander (1901-54) • Catherine Doherty (1896-1985), *Poustinia* (1975) • Mother Teresa of Calcutta (1910-97) **Modern Spiritual Movements** Predominantly lay movements, focusing on the call to holiness and renewal; generally drawing together contemplation with action (evangelization, social justice, etc.); many focus on navigating the path to holiness within secular culture. Became increasingly popular after the Second Vatican Council and its teaching on the Universal Call to Holiness Some of the more prominent examples are below along with the founders, country of origin, and founding year: • Schoenstatt Movement (Fr. Joseph Kentenich, Germany, 1914) • Opus Dei (Fr. Josemaría Escrivá, Spain, 1928) • Catholic Worker Movement (Dorothy Day and Peter Maurin, United States, 1933) • Focolare Movement (Chiara Lubich, Italy, 1943) • Cursillo Movement (group of laymen, Spain, 1944)

	East	West
1917 – Today		• *Comunione e Liberazione* (Fr. Luigi Guissani, Italy, 1954) • *Regnum Christi* (Fr. Marcial Maciel, LC, Mexico, 1959) • Neocatechumenal Way (*Redemptoris Mater*) (two laypeople, Spain, 1964) • Catholic Charismatic Renewal (two laymen, United States, 1967) • Sant'Egidio Community (group of high school students, Italy, 1968) • Families of Nazareth Movement (Fr. Tadeusz Dajczer, Poland, 1985) • Center for Contemplation and Action (Fr. Richard Rohr, OFM, United States, 1986) • ACTS Missions (three laymen, United States, 1986) – offshoot from the Cursillo Movement

The roots of the Church are very deep. For more than two thousand years, prayer has nourished the life of the saints and all the disciples of Jesus. The above analysis demonstrates how the Eastern Christian spiritual tradition has essentially revolved around the Jesus Prayer, beginning with the Desert Fathers and Mothers, and continuing to modern times. Thus, this mystical tradition of the Christian East has been faithfully practiced and preserved since the time of the Early Church.

In contrast, a number of spiritual traditions emerged over time in the West. During the Scholastic Period, there was essentially a separation between theology and spirituality as the study of theology migrated from the monasteries to universities, where it became a field of rigorous academic study. The same separation did not occur in the Christian East, wherein knowledge of God was based on actual experience. The maxim of Evagrius Ponticus is often quoted: "If you are a theologian you truly pray. If you truly pray you are a theologian."[356]

A significant shift occurred at the Second Vatican Council, which espoused *ressourcement*—a return to the sources. This generally meant a shift away from Scholasticism with a renewed emphasis on Sacred Scripture and the Patristic sources. The writings of Karl Rahner, SJ, for example, reflect this shift: "The devout Christian of the future will either be a 'mystic,' one who has 'experienced' something, or he [she] will cease to be anything at all."[357]

The great beauty of the Universal Catholic Church is that it includes the spiritual patrimony of both East and West. Pope St. John Paul II believed the Church needed to learn to breathe again from both lungs, one Eastern and one Western.[358] Recent popes have described the need to rediscover the treasures of the Eastern Catholic Churches in order to create a true synthesis reflective of the Universal Catholic Church. On a similar note, Cardinal Sarah writes, "The spiritual and cultural heritage of the Russian Orthodox Church is unequaled. The reawakening of faith that followed the fall of Communism is an immense hope. It is the fruit of the blood of martyrs."[359] Further, "in Russia, the Orthodox Church has to a great extent resumed its pre-1917 role as the moral foundation of society."[360] One could make similar observations about the Church in Ukraine, Slovakia, Hungary, and Romania, essentially arising from the catacombs, having remained alive and vibrant during Communist repression and preserving the deposit of faith, often at great price. These Eastern

---

356 Evagrius Ponticus, *The Praktikos & Chapters on Prayer*, 65.
357 Karl Rahner, "Christian Living Formerly and Today," in *Theological Investigations*, vol. VII (New York: Seabury Press, 1972), 15.
358 Pope St. John Paul II often spoke of the need for the Church to achieve its deepest meaning by breathing from both its lungs, one Eastern and one Western. See for example *Ut Unum Sint* (Rome: Libreria Editrice Vaticana, 1995), no. 54.
359 Robert Cardinal Sarah, *The Day is Now Far Spent*, 239.
360 Ibid., 240.

Christian experiences and perspectives provide a further richness to our Catholic faith, especially related to mysticism, the theology of encounter, and the hesychast prayer tradition (Jesus Prayer, also known as Prayer of the Heart). Encounter is essential to establishing a deep-seated relationship with Jesus Christ, the source of life, hope, and way to eternal blessedness.

With this emphasis on encounter, we begin to appreciate the spirituality of people like Mother Teresa of Calcutta, who asks us the right question, "Do you really know the living Jesus—not from books but from being with him in your heart?"[361] Her entire apostolate to the poor and suffering was anchored in contemplative prayer. Thus, we come back to our opening thoughts in the introduction about the spiritual journey: to know God's plan for us, we must come to know and love his Son, Jesus Christ. Recall the teaching of Isaac the Syrian, "You cannot taste honey by reading a book." To know Jesus is to experience him.

For further information and a concise history of Christian spirituality including Protestant traditions, we recommend the following:

Sheldrake, Philip. *Spirituality: A Concise History*. 2nd ed. West Sussex, UK: John Wiley-Blackwell, 2013.

---

361 Mother Teresa, "Jesus is My All," edited by Fr. Brian Kolodiejchuk, MC (San Diego, CA: Mother Teresa Center, 2005), 13.

The Rest of the Story

Whatever happened to Teresa? In our first conference in one of the reflections, we introduced Teresa, who wanted to find love and was thirsting for happiness. She was torn between the party scene and prayer meetings, trying to hold on to both worlds. Since this retreat is about choosing life in Christ and radical choices, let us consider the rest of her story.

In her own words, she said, "I wanted both worlds. But I soon began to be disillusioned about the whole party scene and began to feel some remorse for my sinful lifestyle."[362] Going on a visit to Franciscan University in Steubenville and pilgrimage to ETWN and Caritas, Alabama, she desired to follow Jesus, making dramatic changes in her life. As she wrote:

> Needless to say, my conversion to a Christian lifestyle left my friends very bewildered. Once when I met one of my "good ole friends" a couple years later, he looked on me with such disgust, as if he could hardly refrain from spitting in my face! It was difficult at times and I spent many a lonely Friday and Saturday night at home in my room. Yet, at the same time I was grateful for the Lord's mercy and for drawing me into a personal friendship with him.[363]

The thought of a religious vocation was also rekindled (something she thought about as a child in grade school). Teresa took two years off from her studies to work in NET ministries. Then

---

362 https://www.passionistnuns.org/blog/2018/2/16/from-prom-queen-to-cloistered-nun.
363 Ibid.

in January 1995, she describes herself as having struggled for months with returning to college, unable to find peace. She felt she was wasting time and had no desire for a career. Teresa spent a great deal of time in prayer, torn between the desire to find a good husband and get married or to follow Jesus in a different direction. A particular proverb became her constant prayer: "Trust in the Lord with all your heart; lean not on your own understanding. In all your ways acknowledge him and he will direct your paths" (Proverbs 3:5-6).[364]

Based on this, Teresa made a leap of faith and quit school. She said she was flooded with peace. However, as she wrote,

> I think others thought I had gone off the deep end. I even began to wonder if I *had* gone crazy, but I put my trust in Luke 5:1-11. '…when they brought their boats to shore, they left everything and followed him.' I just wanted to follow Jesus![365]

In August 1995, Teresa entered the Passionist Monastery of St. Joseph in Whitesville, Kentucky. In 2016, Sr. John Mary of the Indwelling Trinity, CP, was elected Mother Superior of her community (reelected in 2019), where she resides today.

Mother John Mary made the radical choice to follow Jesus, just like the apostles who got out of the boat, leaving everything behind. She chose to pursue her vocation to holiness, her life in Christ, as a cloistered nun.

---

364 Ibid.

365 Sr. John Mary, "A Life from Prom Queen to Cloistered Nun," http://www.passionistnuns. org/ vocationstories/findinglove/index.htm.

Bibliography

Allen, Joseph J. *The Ministry of the Church: The Image of Pastoral Care*. Crestwood, NY: St. Vladimir's Seminary Press, 1986.

An Ascetic Bishop: Stories, Sermons, and Prayers of St. Nephon. 2nd ed. Translated by Jeannie Gentithes and Archimandrite Ignatios Apostololopoulos. Florence, AZ: St. Anthony's Monastery. 2015.

Art of Prayer, The. Compiled by Igumen Chariton. Translated by E. Kadloubovsky and G. E. H. Palmer. London: Farrar, Straus and Giroux, 1966.

Arthington, Madeline and Karrie Sparrow. "What Happened to the Seven Churches of Revelation?" *International Mission Board* (June 1, 2018). www.imb.org.

Ascetical Homilies of Saint Isaac the Syrian, The. Translated by Holy Transfiguration Monastery. 2nd rev. ed. Brookline, MA: Holy Transfiguration Monastery, 2011.

Augustine of Hippo, St. "Sermon 174.3." Taken from "Luke." Edited by Arthur J. Just, Jr. From *Ancient Christian Commentary on Scripture*, vol. 3. Downers Grove, IL: InterVarsity Press, 2003. 291.

Barry, William A., SJ, *Finding God in All Things*. Notre Dame, IN: Ave Maria Press, 1991.

Benedict XVI, Pope. *Porta Fidei*. Rome: Libreria Editrice Vaticana, 2011.

Bonhoeffer, Dietrich *The Cost of Discipleship*. New York: Simon & Schuster, 1995.

Breck, John. "Prayer of the Heart: Sacrament of the Presence of God," *St. Vladimir's Theological Quarterly* 29, no. 1 (1995): 25–45.

Bunge, Gabriel, OSB. *Earthen Vessels: The Practice of Personal Prayer According to the Patristic Tradition.* San Francisco, CA: Ignatius Press, 2002.

Catholic News Service. "Young Adults Want to be Heard by the Church, Study Finds." *Texas Catholic Herald,* January 23, 2018.

Chaput, Charles J., OFM Cap. *Living the Catholic Faith: Rediscovering the Basics.* Cincinnati, OH: St. Anthony Messenger Press, 2001.

———. *Strangers in a Strange Land: Practicing the Catholic Faith in a Post-Christian World.* New York: Henry Holt, 2017.

Charron, Fr. Jason. Carnegie, PA: Holy Trinity Ukrainian Catholic Church website. http://www. http://htucc.com.

"Church on Mission, The" *Magnificat,* 21, no. 8 (2019): 174.

Chrysostom, St. John. "Homily on Matthew 15." Taken from *The Liturgy of the Hours,* vol. IV. New York: Catholic Book Publishing Co., 1975. 120-122.

Chryssavgis, John. *In the Heart of the Desert: The Spirituality of the Desert Fathers and Mothers.* Bloomington, IN: World Wisdom, Inc., 2003.

Climacus, St. John. *The Ladder of Divine Ascent.* Translated by Colm Luibheid and Norman Russell. New York: Paulist Press, 1982.

Coniaris, Anthony M. *Tools for Theosis: Becoming God-like in Christ.* Minneapolis, MN: Light & Life Publishing Company, 2014.

Damascene, Hieromonk. *Father Seraphim Rose: His Life and His Works.* 3rd rev. ed. Platina, CA: St. Herman of Alaska Brotherhood, 2010.

Davies, Hieromonk Maximos. "Lenten Mission 2018: Hope." Delivered at St. Sophia Ukrainian Greek Catholic Church, The Colony, Texas, February 23-25, 2018.

Deacon and Fellow Pilgrim, A. *Hearts Afire: A Personal Encounter with Jesus.* 2nd ed. Fairfax, VA: Eastern Christian Publications, 2016.

———. *Hearts Afire: Fulfilling Our Destiny*. 2nd printing. Fairfax, VA: Eastern Christian Publications, 2014.

Didache, The: The Teaching of the Twelve Apostles. Translated by R. Joseph Owles. (North Charleston, SC: CreateSpace, 2014.

DiNardo, Daniel Cardinal, "A Catechetical Framework for Lifelong Faith Formation," Archdiocese of Galveston-Houston, Office of Catechesis and Evangelization (August 6, 2013).

Divine Liturgies of Our Holy Father John Chrysostom, The. Pittsburgh, PA: Byzantine Seminary Press, 2006,

Dorotheos of Gaza. *Discourses and Sayings*. Translated by Eric P. Wheeler. Kalamazoo, MI: Cistercian Publications, 1977.

Evagrius Ponticus. *The Praktikos & Chapters on Prayer*. Translated by John Eudes Bamberger, OCSO. Kalamazoo, MI: Cistercian Publications, 1972.

Francis, Pope. Address. Meeting with the Bishops of Brazil (July 28, 2013).

———. *Evangelii Gaudium*. Rome: Libreria Editrice Vaticana, 2013.

———. *Gaudete et Exsultate*. Rome: Libreria Editrice Vaticana, 2019.

———. "The Grace that Overcomes Duplicity," *Magnificat*, 21, no. 6 (2019): 354-355.

George, Archimandrite. *Theosis: The True Purpose of Human Life*. Mount Athos: Holy Monastery of St. Gregorios, 2006.

Gregory of Nyssa, St. "On the Beatitudes." *Ancient Christian Writers: The Works of the Fathers in Translation,* vol. 18, 85-175. Edited by Johannes Quasten and Joseph C. Plumpe, transl. Hilda C. Graef. New York: Paulist Press, 1954.

Heneghan, Tom. "Dutch Bishops Give Pope Francis a Bleak Picture of the Catholic Church in Decline." *FaithWorld*. Reuters Online. December 3, 2013.

Hierotheos of Nafpaktos, Metropolitan. *A Night in the Desert of the Holy Mountain: Discussion with a Hermit on the Jesus Prayer*. Translated by Effie Mavromichali. Levadia, Greece: Birth of the Theotokos Monastery, 2009.

John of Kronstadt, St. *My Life in Christ*, Part 1. Part 1 and Part 2. Translated by E. E. Goulaeff. Revised and adapted by Nicholas Kotar. Jordanville, NY: Holy Trinity Monastery, 2015.

———. *The Spiritual Counsels of Fr. John of Kronstadt.* Edited by W. Jardine Grisbrooke. Crestwood, NY: St. Vladimir's Seminary Press, 1981.

John Mary, Sr. "A Life from Prom Queen to Cloistered Nun." http://www.passionistnuns.org/vocationstories/findinglove/index.htm.

John Paul II, Pope St. *Novo Millennio Ineunte*. Rome: Libreria Editrice Vaticana, 2001.

Johnson, Luke Timothy. *The Gospel of Luke*. Taken from Sacra Pagina series, vol. 3. Edited by Daniel J. Harrington, SJ. Collegeville, MN: The Liturgical Press, 1991.

Kaisch, Ken. *Finding God: A Handbook of Christian Meditation*. New York: Paulist Press, 1994.

Keating, Thomas, OCSO. *Intimacy with God*. New York: The Crossroad Publishing Company, 2002.

Keller, David G. R. *Desert Banquet: A Year of Wisdom from the Desert Mothers and Fathers*. Collegeville, MN: Liturgical Press, 2011.

———. *Oasis of Wisdom: The Worlds of the Desert Fathers and Mothers*. Collegeville, MN: Liturgical Press, 2005.

Kelly, Matthew. *Rediscover Jesus*. Ellicott City, MD: Beacon Publishing, 2015.

———. *Rediscover the Saints*. Assam, India: Blue Sparrow Books, 2019.

Kleinguetl, Edward. *Encounter: Experiencing the Divine Presence*. Parker CO: Outskirts Press, 2018.

Kerul-Kmec, Rev. Miron. Homily. St. Nicholas Byzantine Catholic Church, Barberton, Ohio (June 23, 2019). https://artofspirituallife.podbean.com/e/june-23-2019-1561584878/.

———. Homily. St. Nicholas Byzantine Catholic Church, Barberton, Ohio (September 1, 2019). https://artofspirituallife.podbean.com/e/september-1-2019-1567374085/.

Lach, Most Rev. Milan, SJ. "A Year of Renewal." Pastoral Letter to the Faithful of the Byzantine Catholic Eparchy of Parma (January 6, 2019).

Langford, Joseph, MC. *Mother Teresa's Secret Fire*. Huntington, IN: Our Sunday Visitor, 2008.

Lewis, C.S. *Mere Christianity*. New York: Macmillan. 1952.

Maloney, George, SJ. *Prayer of the Heart: The Contemplative Tradition of the Christian East*. Notre Dame, IN: Ave Maria Press, 2008.

Marmion, Blessed Columba. "Giving without Cost," *Magnificat*, 21, no. 5 (2019): 157-158.

Monk of Mount Athos, A. *The Watchful Mind: Teachings on the Prayer of the Heart*. Translated by George Dokos. Yonkers, NY: St. Vladimir's Seminary Press, 2014.

Moses, Monk, of Mount Athos. *Athonite Flowers: Seven Contemporary Essays on the Spiritual Life*. Translated by Fr. Peter A. Chamberas. Brookline, MA: Holy Cross Press, 2000.

———. *Holiness: Is It Attainable Today?* Translated by Fr. Peter A. Chamberas. Brookline, MA: Holy Cross Orthodox Press, 2012.

Murray, Fr. Gerald E. Murray, "Cardinal Sarah and Our Silent Apostasy," *The Catholic Thing* (Jan. 16, 2016).

Nolan, Albert. *Jesus Before Christianity*. Maryknoll, NY: Orbis Books, 2013.

Paul VI, Pope St. *Evangelii Nuntiandi*. Rome: Libreria Editrice Vaticana, 1975.

Pilgrim's Tale, The. Translated by T. Allan Smith. "Introduction" by Aleksei Pentkovsky. Mahwah, NJ: Paulist Press, 1999.

Pope, Charles Pope, "Comfort Catholicism Has to Go; It is Time to Prepare for Persecution." *National Catholic Register* online (August 21, 2016). www. http://m.ncregister.com/blog/msgr-pope/comfort-catholicism-has-to-go-it-is-time-to-prepare-for-persecution?fbclid=IwAR12Uo43mGzp1EymdNRZ5LHJrgWj nmmrpeJ-VM8ZvR6Y5HPq6nv0-i5BYA.

Porphyrios, Elder. *Wound by Love: The Life and Wisdom of Elder Porphyrios*. Edited by Sisters of the Holy Convent of Chrysopigi. Translated by John Raffan. Limni, Evia, Greece: Denise Harvey, 2013.

Pronechen, Joseph. "Archbishop Sheen's Warning of a Crisis in Christendom." *National Catholic Register*. Online Edition. July 29, 2018.

Rahner, Karl, SJ. "Christian Living Formerly and Today," *Theological Investigations*, vol. VII. New York: Seabury Press, 1972.

Rohr, Richard, OFM. "Breathing Under Water," *St. Anthony Messenger* (August 2019): 33-38.

Sakharov, Archimandrite Sophrony. *St. Silouan the Athonite*. Translated by Rosemary Edmonds. Crestwood, NY: St. Vladimir's Seminary Press, 1991.

————. *We Shall See Him As He Is*. Platina, CA; St. Herman of Alaska Brotherhood, 2006.

Sarah, Robert Cardinal, in conversation with Nicolas Diat. *God or Nothing: A Conversation on Faith*. Translated by Michael J. Miller. San Francisco, CA: Ignatius Press, 2015.

————. *The Day is Now Far Spent*. Translated by Michael J. Miller. San Francisco, CA: Ignatius Press, 2019.

————. "You follow me," *Magnificat*, 19, no. 4 (2017): 54.

Sayings of the Desert Fathers, The. Translated by Benedicta Ward, SLG. Kalamazoo, MI: Cistercian Publications, 1975.

Sheldrake, Philip. *Spirituality: A Concise History*. 2nd ed. West Sussex, UK: John Wiley-Blackwell, 2013.

Smith, Peter. "Catholic Panel Recommends Parish Mergers." *Pittsburgh Post-Gazette*, Sept. 16, 2017.

Stavropoulos, Archimandrite Christoforos. *Partakers of Divine Nature*. Translated by Rev. Dr. Stanley Harakas. Minneapolis, MN: Light & Life Publishing Company, 1976.

Strickland, Bishop Joseph E. Comments at the USCCB Meeting (November 13, 2018). https://www.youtube.com/watch?v=gsURjhLkvTg.

Teresa, Mother. "Jesus is My All." Edited by Fr. Brian Kolodiejchuk, MC. San Diego, CA: Mother Teresa Center, 2005.

———. *Love: A Fruit Always in Season*. Edited by Dorothy S. Hunt. San Francisco, CA: Ignatius Press, 1987.

Tertullian. *Apologeticum*. Taken from "Tertullian's Defense." Translated by Rev. S. Thelwall. Modernized by Stephen Tomkins. Edited by Dan Graves. www.christianhistoryinstitute.org/study/module/tertullian.

United States Catholic Conference of Bishops. Committee on Evangelization and Catechesis. *Disciples Called to Witness: The New Evangelization*. Washington, DC, 2013.

Unseen Warfare. Being the "Spiritual Combat" and "Path to Paradise" of Lorenzo Scupoli. Edited by Nicodemus of the Holy Mountain. Revised by Theophan the Recluse. Translated by E. Kadloubovsky and G. E. H. Palmer. Crestwood, NY: St. Vladimir's Seminary Press, 1963.

Ware, Kallistos. *The Philokalia: Master Reference Guide*. Compiled by Basileios S. Stapkis. Edited by Gerald Eustace Howell Palmer and Philip Sherrard. Minneapolis, MN: Light & Life Publishing Company, 2004.

Weigel, George. "Eastern Catholics and the Universal Church." *First Things* online (June 6, 2019). www.firstthings.com/web-exclusive/2019/06/eastern-catholics-and-the-universal-church.

Zander, Valentine, *St. Seraphim of Sarov*. Translated by Sr. Gabriel Anne, SSC. Crestwood, NY: St. Vladimir's Seminary Press, 1975.

Acknowledgments

This work is inspired by a number of people and sources. First, I would like to acknowledge His Grace Bishop Milan Lach, SJ of the Eparchy of Parma (Ruthenian Byzantine Catholic), who joyously answered the call to serve Christ and said "yes" to serve in the United States. As part of the 50-year anniversary celebrating the establishment of the eparchy this year, he has called the faithful to a year of spiritual renewal. He says his primary role as bishop is to teach his people how to pray. He is committed to a revival of interest in the Church Fathers, helping others to discover or be renewed in the Art of Spiritual Life, including ascetical practices and learning how to pray in the tradition of the Eastern Church Fathers (Jesus Prayer). We pray that he will be the spark to set the earth on fire (Luke 12:49), because the American Church desperately needs the spiritual treasures of the Eastern Catholic Churches, particularly its mystical spiritual tradition of encounter and *theosis*. The people of the United States need these treasures too, because they provide answers for those who are searching for meaning or purpose, those who are drifting and despairing. We pray that your zeal for renewal and drawing people into a deeper relationship with Christ will never fade, and to persevere when the mission or challenges seem overwhelming. Thank you for your "yes" to come to the United States. This book is dedicated to you in grateful appreciation and thanksgiving.

This retreat is the culmination of a series of books, all of which have been themed around the Eastern Christian doctrine of *theosis*. This is the incremental process of transformation, becoming more Christ-like, preparing ourselves for our ultimate destiny—eternal blessedness (union with God). The initial inspiration for the first book, a graduate school thesis that provided the theological framework for the other works, was His Grace Bishop John M. Kudrick, Bishop Emeritus of the Eparchy of Parma. He had a great desire for his flock to be well-grounded in the beauty of their heritage and, when he expressed a desire to have an "Americanized" version of the *Theosis* Retreats, this entire effort was set into motion. Your Grace, the Church desperately needs true spiritual fathers like you, holy men who can lead us closer to Christ.

I would like to thank His Grace Archbishop Charles J. Chaput, OFM Cap of Philadelphia, whose books *Living the Catholic Faith* and *Strangers in a Strange Land* have been a great source of inspiration. His Grace remains a constant voice against complacency in the American Church and is continuously recognized as one of the most trusted and admired bishops of our time. Similarly, His Eminence Robert Cardinal Sarah has been an outspoken voice against deviations from orthodox teaching. His books *God or Nothing* and *The Day is Now Far Spent* have influenced this work. Thank you, both, for courageously speaking with clarity at a time when the Church most needs it.

His Excellency Bishop Joseph E. Strickland of Tyler is another courageous voice, who in his address to the bishops at the USCCB meeting in Baltimore in November 2018 remarked, "Jesus Christ brings Good News to the world." When he spoke of the atmosphere over the youth synod in Rome,[366] he said he heard a lot about "confusion and difficulty," but he "did not hear much about the Good News of the Gospel of Jesus Christ; he lived, died, and rose so that we could be free from sin and death." He told his fellow bishops that the more they can share the Good News, the more we can overcome our current challenges. We concur with his sentiments and, we hope, *Choosing Life in Christ* becomes part of that effort to bring the Good News of the Gospel to the world. Thank you, Your Excellency, for not being silent when the Church needs the voice of its shepherds to speak with clarity.

---

366 XV Ordinary General Assembly of the Synod of Bishops, "Young People, the Faith, and Vocational Discernment," Oct. 3-28, 2018.

Acknowledgments

I would like to acknowledge and thank Fr. Miron Kerul-Kmec for his continuous support, encouragement, and spiritual counsel. He has a great desire to lead his community closer to Christ by guiding them in terms of the interior life (the Art of Spiritual Life), reflecting on the teachings of the Eastern Fathers of the Church. He is a true shepherd and spiritual father who epitomizes my favorite model of Church, *sobornost*—the church at the center of the village, drawing all people together, a beacon of light and hope. Just as God should be at the center of our lives, so should the parish church be at the heart of our communities. Fr. Miron's passion for evangelization has greatly inspired me during the past six years. He recognizes the true mission of a parish community: to help its members come to know and love Jesus Christ, preparing them for the life that is to come. A friend who does not know him listened to one of his homilies via podcast and said it best: "This is a priest who cares deeply for his people." How true! The theme of this retreat was inspired by his homily delivered on June 23, 2019, and his input has been invaluable. While the challenges of evangelization in light of the dominant culture are great, I pray that you never lose your zeal for the salvation of souls. You are a great spiritual father. I am so grateful to Fr. Miron, his wife Marcelka, and the members of St. Nicholas Byzantine Catholic Church in Barberton, Ohio, for being such a welcoming community. They are proof of what a vibrant parish can truly be like.

Subdeacon Miron Kerul-Kmec, Jr., is an amazing iconographer and will be an excellent priest; he understands the importance of the interior life and helping people experience the Risen Jesus. Given responsibility for the eparchial youth retreat in 2020, Miron asked me for some thoughts, which provided the inspiration to create this work. The Church needs true spiritual fathers and, like his own father, I am certain Miron will be one. The journey has not been an easy one. However, suffering perfects our faith and prepares us for the road ahead. May Christ continue to form you after his own heart, may the Holy Spirit direct your steps, and may the wisdom of the Church

Fathers provide the example of perseverance in imitation of Christ. Also, I want to acknowledge his fiancée and future *presbytera*, Sarah Marie, and wish both of you much success and many blessings in your joint vocation. Thank you for your friendship and making me feel like part of your family.

I am also grateful to Donna Rueby, who envisioned the importance of planting and nurturing the seed of faith in our high school youth. Through a series of experiential retreats, the "Surfside Beach Retreats," she created an opportunity for our young people to have a genuine encounter with Christ, in the hope that such an experience would create deeper roots for their faith before going off to college. Also, I want to thank Fr. Arthur Carrillo, CP, with whom I worked on several of these retreats, and who taught me much about creating an impactful, cohesive retreat. He also provided some excellent insights to an early manuscript of this retreat.

Thank you to Fr. Mark Goring, CC, for his passion for evangelization, especially through his YouTube videos. He is outspoken about the truth of the Gospel, encouraging others to deepen their spiritual life, and to the pursuit of virtue. *¡Viva Christo Rey!*

Thank you to Fr. Luke Millette, who is a true model of pastoral care and concern. Too few priests possess your compassion for the plight of others. I will always be grateful for your counsel and wisdom.

Others also encouraged me on my spiritual journey: My priest-mentor, Fr. Edward Zavell, adopted me as a young man in high school seminary and inflamed my passion for Byzantine Catholicism. And, where would one be in the Eastern Christian spiritual tradition without an outstanding Spiritual Father? For me, that person is Fr. Damon Geiger, who was my spiritual guide during my first three years of ordained ministry. He helped me delve much more deeply into the beauty of the Eastern Christian mystical tradition and first introduced me to the concept of *theosis*. What Fr. Ed planted, Fr. Damon cultivated by opening my eyes to the true beauty that lay beneath the ornate liturgies and traditions.

Our youth are the future of our Church, the ones to whom we are entrusted to pass along our spiritual treasures. They truly desire to know how to pray and to understand the Catholic faith they profess. Similarly, I want to acknowledge the efforts of the Eparchy of Passaic and Fr. Deacon Tom Shubeck for their focus on engaging young adults through the program, *Theosis in Action*. On August 1-4, 2019, this eparchy hosted a convocation of young adults in New York entitled "Called. Transfigured. Sent." This encompassed a few of the same themes contained herein.

Speaking of prayer, I am grateful to the sisters of the Carmel Monastery of the Holy Trinity in New Caney, Texas, who regularly pray for me. In particular, I am grateful to Sr. Josefina of the Trinity, OCD, and Sr. Mary Thérèse of the Eucharist, OCD, who encourage me to write. Of course, there is also Mother John Mary, CP of the Passionist Nuns at St. Joseph Monastery in Whitesville, Kentucky, whose story of "prom queen to cloistered nun" is a reminder of what it means to say "yes," making the radical choice to follow Christ. Thank you for your witness and prayers.

Finally, there were many others along the journey who provided input, inspiration, proofreading, and other helpful suggestions and support. I would specifically like to thank Gene Kirsch for his passion and enthusiasm in presenting his own witness about developing a personal relationship with God and perspectives on prayer.

The title of this retreat was in no small part influenced by the spiritual diary of St. John of Kronstadt (1829-1908), which was published as *My Life in Christ*.

To all the servants of God who influenced this work—His Eminence Cardinal Sarah, His Grace Archbishop Charles, His Grace Bishop Milan, His Grace Bishop John, His Excellency Bishop Joseph, Fr. Miron, Pani Marcelka, Subdeacon Miron, Jr., future *presbytera* Sarah

Marie, the parishioners of St. Nicholas Byzantine Catholic Church in Barberton, Ohio, Fr. Arthur, Fr. Mark, Fr. Luke, Fr. Damon, Fr. Deacon Tom, Mother John Mary, Sr. Josefina, Sr. Mary Thérèse, Donna, the youth and young adults who desire to enter into a deeper relationship with Jesus Christ, Gene and his daughters Kathrine, Nicole, and Kimberly, and all others, too numerous to mention — may God grant you many blessed years in peace, health, and happiness. *Mnohaja I blahaja lita.*

To my priest-mentor, Fr. Ed, may God grant him eternal memory and blessed repose. *Vičnaja jemu pamjat'.*

Fr. Deacon Edward Kleinguetl
Fr. Deacon Edward Kleinguetl, MASp
September 14, 2019
Feast of the Exaltation of the Holy Cross

"Save your people, O Lord, and bless your inheritance. Grant victory to your Church over evil, and protect your people by your cross."

—Troparion of the Cross

"Salve Crux Spes Unica"
("Hail the Cross, Our Only Hope")

—Episcopal Motto
Daniel Cardinal DiNardo
Archbishop of Galveston-Houston

Other Resources Available

(Listed in chronological order based on first edition)

A Deacon and Fellow Pilgrim. *Hearts Afire: A Personal Encounter with Jesus.* 2nd ed. Fairfax, VA: Eastern Christian Publications, 2016.

> Discusses the ancient practice of the Jesus Prayer. Available in English and Spanish at www.ecpubs.com. Imprimatur for both translations: His Eminence Daniel Cardinal DiNardo, Archbishop of Galveston-Houston.

A Deacon and Fellow Pilgrim. *Hearts Afire: Fulfilling Our Destiny.* 2nd ed. Fairfax, VA: Eastern Christian Publications, 2016.

> Discusses regaining the likeness of God (*theosis*) by reviewing selected passages of Sacred Scripture through a series of conferences and discussion questions. Available at www.ecpubs.com. Imprimatur: His Grace Bishop John Kudrick, Bishop Emeritus of the Eparchy of Parma (Ruthenian Byzantine Catholic).

Edward Kleinguetl. *Fulfilling Our Destiny: Theosis, Pope Francis, and the Jubilee of Mercy.* Jan. 2016.

> Parish Mission delivered at St. Nicholas Byzantine Catholic Church, Barberton, Ohio. Explores the Eastern Christian Doctrine of Theosis through the lens of Pope Francis's writings, especially *Evangelii Gaudium* and *Misericordiae Vultus.*
>
> Available online only at http://www.stnickbyz.com/pub/doc/archive/fod_retreat.pdf.

Edward Kleinguetl. *Encounter: Experiencing the Risen Jesus, Fulfilling Our Deepest Longing.* North Charleston, SC: CreateSpace, 2017.

> A theological framework considering the relevance of faith through a "spirituality of encounter." Available both in paperback or Kindle at www.amazon.com. Imprimatur: His Eminence Daniel Cardinal DiNardo, Archbishop of Galveston-Houston.

Edward Kleinguetl. *Encounter: Experiencing the Risen Jesus (A Retreat).* North Charleston, SC: CreateSpace, 2017.

> A four-conference retreat addressing our ability to encounter the divine presence.

Edward Kleinguetl. *Journey: Striving for Our Destiny*. North Charleston, SC: CreateSpace, 2017.

> Series of reflections on the ups and downs of the spiritual journey using the context of Holy Week. Imprimatur: His Eminence Daniel Cardinal DiNardo, Archbishop of Galveston-Houston.

Edward Kleinguetl. *Encounter: Experiencing the Divine Presence*. Parker, CO: Outskirts Press, 2018.

> A series of conversations examining critical aspects of our faith by focusing on our experiences of encounters with the divine presence. Enriched by the Church's Eastern Christian patrimony, which retains a mystical tradition centered on the interior life and contemplative prayer. Imprimatur: His Eminence Daniel Cardinal DiNardo, Archbishop of Galveston-Houston.

Edward Kleinguetl. *Into the Desert: The Wisdom of the Desert Fathers and Mothers*. Parker, CO: Outskirts Press, 2019.

> A series of conferences structured as a retreat focusing on tried and true lessons from the Early Desert Dwellers, who modeled a very back-to-basics spirituality focused on cultivating a relationship with God. The lessons of the desert are equally relevant to today as they were in the ancient times of the Church. Available both in paperback and Kindle at www.amazon.com. Imprimatur: His Eminence Daniel Cardinal DiNardo, Archbishop of Galveston-Houston.

CPSIA information can be obtained
at www.ICGtesting.com
Printed in the USA
FFHW012103111119
56027455-61947FF